A Lang Way
to the Pawnshop

(Helping to Make Ends Meet)

THOMAS CALLAGHAN

LARGE PRINT
Oxford

Copyright © Zymurgy Publishing, 2001

First published in Great Britain 1978 by Frank Graham

Published in Large Print 2003 by ISIS Publishing Ltd,
7 Centremead, Osney Mead, Oxford OX2 0ES
by arrangement with Zymurgy Publishing

British Library Cataloguing in Publication Data
Callaghan, Thomas, 1924–
  A lang way to the pawnshop. – Large print ed.
  (Isis reminiscence series)
  1. Callaghan, Thomas, 1924– – Childhood
  and youth
  2. Large type books
  3. England, Northern – Social life and customs
  – 20th century
  4. England, Northern – Social conditions
  – 20th century
  5. England, Northern – Biography
  I. Title
  942.7'083'092

ISBN 0–7531–9870–3 (hb)
ISBN 0–7531–9871–1 (pb)

Printed and bound by Antony Rowe, Chippenham

Dedicated to my parents
and to
Vera and Frank Graham

Contents

Author's Note

Some of the names of characters in this book are fictitious.

For the benefit of the uninitiated who would probably have difficulty in comprehension, I have not strictly adhered to the Tyneside dialect.

Chapter 11, "Paddy's Market", was adapted as a six part serial in November–December, 1976, and broadcast by B.B.C. Radio Newcastle.

A few excerpts from part of this book, including the whole of the final chapter, was published in March, 1976, by Blackwoods Magazine, Edinburgh.

Preface

I wrote this book, mentally at least three years before I put pen to paper! The title of it was, "Helping to Make Ends Meet". It was the late Sid Chaplin, who on reading the manuscript suggested the eye-catching title of "A Lang Way To The Pawnshop". In the book I mention the Charity Treats to South Shields during summer school holidays and organised by the offices of The Poor Children's Holiday Association. As we lads and lasses marched down towards Elswick Railway Station on Scotswood Road, we would begin singing our usual vocal to the tune of "It's A Long Way to Tipperary":

> It's a lang way to the pawnshop
> It's a lang way to gan.
> It's a lang way to the pawnshop,
> Where all the mothers gan.
> Farewell coat and waistcoat,
> Farewell watch and chain.
> And if a divn't keep an eye on me troosers,
> They'll gan the same.

I found no difficulty writing the book, how could I? I had lived through every sequence of it. My adventures, experiences and the task of making a few coppers to assist in helping to make ends meet, were those of many another lad whether it be in Benwell, Scotswood or Elswick. I came across very few bored kids during my boyhood, we all organised our own pastimes, so apart from running messages, there was little time or patience to sit twiddling one's thumbs; to manage a penny for the Cinema Matinee was all we looked forward to, which was often difficult to get, unless delivering and selling newspapers, or hawking firewood round the posh parts of Benwell. The only thing that was missing in those days for many of us was the total lack of funds due mainly to unemployment. Poverty was responsible for cramped living space, second-hand clothes and footwear, and an adequate diet to keep one healthy.

Today things are improved for many: housing, and a better education. Yet for a large minority, the poverty trap keeps them isolated from sharing in the improvement that had come about in the last thirty years or so. I seldom see children playing the same games as we did during the 20s and 30s. There being no television those days, and sometime not even a wireless, there was more scope, and necessity to employ one's imagination. We made our own entertainment without the aid of videos, computers and TV games — some of which appear mindless and too competitive. All being produced in our space age era, by those who are more concerned solely with profit than offering wholesome entertainment.

Tom Callaghan, June 2001

Introduction

This is the best "read" I have come across on the subject of growing up in Newcastle upon Tyne since Kiddar's Luck, although it has, of course, the advantage of filling in the gap between the late 1920s (where Common left it), and the outbreak of the Second World War.

It is also about the downgraded West End (specifically Benwell village), and deals with another social stratum altogether. Where Common deals with the respectable artisan class, Callaghan is concerned with the very poorest of the poor. So along with a rich portrait gallery of the Benwell poor of those days there are acute and detailed descriptions of what it is like to be desperately hungry, cadgers cadging from cadgers, tatters (freelance scrap merchants) plying their trade along with second-hand clothes dealers like Callaghan's Auntie who, as well as keeping a shop, pushed the pick of her stock-in-trade piled up in a hand-cart to Paddy's Market early every Saturday — to complete with hucksters, tipsters and prostitutes, all equally eager to sell their wares.

Young Tommy occupied a big double bed in their two room flat with his father and three other brothers — and early learned to shift quick of a morning to collect the baker's leavings before he was hooked out by Callaghan Senior's feet. In a world of the permanently

unemployed he learned to fend for himself or else —
and brilliantly succeeded. You might call him a poor
man's George Orwell, only born to it, there was never
any question of his having to find material on what it
was like to be down-and-out in Benwell, or anywhere
else for that matter. And unlike Orwell, he always gets
the infinite graduations of caste within the working
classes exactly right. The "proper" working class didn't
steal for instance, not because it was criminal or against
their religious scruples but simply as matter of sturdy
pride. Yet another obstacle was the cunning and
watchfulness of shop-keepers. Hence our hero refusing
a pair of boots, (his size) abstracted by a drunk from
the entrance to a shop.

He knew, if the drunk didn't, that only odd boots
were hung up on display outside. Pride also made it
"a lang way to the pawnshop" bearing father's suit— a
certainty at seven bob for staving off poverty but only if
you could avoid the cruel-hard "Madame". Tradesmen
(shopfolk) were generally a hard lot, especially the
wives; but there were angels come down to earth in the
shape of a strapping big local baker, and the bonny lass
at the grocers at the corner shop whose departure
meant empty bellies for all of the Callaghans. Pride
stopped only at one point — a free ride. If the tram was
packed and city-bound you could always nip aboard,
taking care to drop off at every stop and re-join again
with the rush of the crowd. In that way you could
actually make it to the city and back: thus breaking out
of prison for a while.

For despite a magnificent tram service, Benwell constituted a veritable ghetto for its inhabitants, who lacked the necessary two or three coppers to take them to its lovely open spaces (Town Moor, Jesmond Dene, Gosforth Park), or within easy reach of the sea. Despite its reliance on family, its espirit de corps and a fighting spirit which made short work of Moseley's Blackshirts, Benwell folk were immobilised by poverty. More and more it came to resemble a prison camp, sans guards, and walls with watch-towers. The dole and the Means Test Man made it so.

The second thing which strikes one about pre-war Benwell is the extraordinary way in which the Victorian work discipline endured in conditions of no settled work. As Callaghan points out, even when the roads were crammed with four-footed traffic — bakers and butchers vans, Rington's Tea horses and massive great brewery beasts, the street sweepers never had occasion to bend their backs, "for the local allotment holders were on continuous patrol with their home-made bogies". With a family of eight, Callaghan Senior had no other option but take up his illegal occupation of "tatting". Nevertheless, he simply couldn't bear being idle, either indoors or outdoors. So also the son. An odd-job man himself from the early age of seven it was his pride and boast to be not only the fastest but the greatest at whatever he undertook — whether scrounging for cheap food, paper-selling or running a firewood business. His favourite cowboy stars no doubt inspired him, but he was also geared by the very same Victorian work concept as his father. But the all-important element which mellows all this is Tom Callaghan's clear-sighted, self-mocking view of himself. Gaiety infuses the book. Where Old Callaghan spouted ill-digested Marxism, the son went out and found fun and enlightenment, even through the worst of his tribulations. If ever I get down to writing my own life story I can only hope that it comes out halfway near as faithful and as full of the joy of celebration as *A Lang Way to the Pawnshop*. Which is not to say that the book is to be taken lightly — if only that in so much of it, engrossing and fascinating as is, the material comes out with a quick kick at the tail end of it. As for instance in his account of the odd-job man "who hung around the market making himself available to any beck-and-call. He would haul a barrow of merchandise from the market to any distance, uphill and downhill, all for a few coppers; yet he never complained of his lot. All he ever expected was a bite to eat, and a kip in the Sally Army; and this was all he ever did get! 'Blessed are the meek, for they shall inherit — bugger all.'" In ten words an epitaph not only for the poor of Benwell Village past, but for all the millions on the dole then — and now.

Sid Chaplin

CHAPTER
ONE

My Neighbourhood

My paternal grandparents, born on Tyneside, were of Irish Catholic stock. My paternal grandfather was a prize-fighter in his younger days; later he became a publican, which he remained to the day he died.

Like a number of prize-fighter publicans in his days, he did not take too kindly to the presence of women on his licensed premises; only charwomen, and those seeking to have their jugs topped-up, were ever allowed into the two houses he managed.

Due apparently to his own strict religious upbringing, he held his own faith, and indeed the religious beliefs of others in contempt.

His wife, was a passive, and rather a pious woman; the mother of three children, two boys and a girl; my father being the youngest of the family. The children's religious upbringing was as to be expected a Catholic one; least that is as far as the instruction they received at school; at home, the religious essence was weakened by the opposition of her husband. At weekends, and on holidays, the children only attended mass when my grandfather was either asleep in bed, or at work; and needless to say, the Parish Priest always ensured that

1

the master of the house was absent from home before making a visit.

My own father once told me, that many a time on returning from mass, and my grandfather realising where he had been, he was rewarded with a clout over the ear; and poor grandmother fared worse for sending him.

My maternal grandfather, was of Scots descent; a miner by profession; and a devout chapel man. He was strict in both his outlook, and habits; but nevertheless a good man, respected by his family, and neighbours. His wife, Elizabeth Devlin, was a native of Dublin. Like many an Irish girl before her time, and since, she left Ireland in her teens to come over to England to be employed in private service. From a maid downstairs, she worked her way upstairs, to become a housekeeper. How she came to meet my grandfather I do not know.

From my mother and her sister, my Aunt Dolly, I learned that the marriage was quite a success for many years. She reared a large family; and as to be expected with her domestic training, she was a model housekeeper, and a good mother.

When my own mother was in her teens, differences developed between her parents. What the main cause was of their separation, none of the children learned; however two of the obvious differences were my maternal grandmother taking to the glass, and the pipe.

Her husband was against all drink; and although he smoked a pipe himself, he was determinedly against his wife enjoying the habit.

Leaving the family home, she once more took to earning her living as housekeeper, a post she held to a good age. She died in the thirties, aged 94; enjoying her noggin and clay pipe to the end.

I was born on the 27th of April, 1924, in Mill Lane, Newcastle upon Tyne; the third son of a family of ten. By the time I had reached my second birthday, we had moved further along the terrace into Benwell.

The reason for moving was a cheaper rent; moving house in those days was a common event for many a family, for living space or rather the amount of it, had often to be sacrificed, for the sake of a reduced rent.

In Benwell, there was the main terrace where all the shopping could be done without spending precious coppers on tram fares going to town in the hope of finding a bargain.

From either side of the terrace ran streets of houses and flats; and in those days, there was a shop on every street corner, most of them general dealers. How on earth they all made a living under such fierce competition was anyone's guess; needless to say there were no fixed time of shop opening, or closing, and you could buy groceries, and pies and peas, up to eleven at night; if you had the money.

Below Benwell, lies Westmorland Road, an area, which during the Victorian era, had been one of the select districts of Newcastle; large houses, with servants in the basements, and up in the attics; but during my childhood, those once luxurious abodes were mostly converted into flats, and furnished rooms, and the less said about the furnishings the better.

3

Below Westmorland Road lies Scotswood Road, that long road that leads to Blaydon; it was about the busiest road in Newcastle then.

There was no shortage of pubs, pawnbrokers, and second-hand shops on it. From Elswick, to Scotswood Bridge on the south side, was occupied mostly by Vickers Armstrongs, a huge factory, which even in those days of long dole queues, employed quite a number of people. Scotswood Road is about three miles long, and in those days there were over eighty pubs on it; no one could pub-crawl along that road and sink a glass of beer at every bar, no matter how solvent they were; though a few hard cases attempted the feat now and then.

There was every conceivable business in operation on that road; including the employment exchange, for what purpose it was serving other than the paying out of meagre benefits.

Up above Benwell is situated the West Road, which could be said, commences at Pilgrim Street in the city, and leads direct to Hexham, and to the remains of Hadrian's Wall.

At the city end of Scotswood Road there was situated the town abattoir. A number of times as a boy I stood in the open doorway of this distasteful building witnessing terror stricken animals being butchered; thank heaven we had others willing to do our dirty work for us.

I remember one cynical old gentleman informing me when I was a lad, and who had observed me coming away from the abattoir, that the building occupied part of the site of the old infirmary which, according to him, had also been a slaughterhouse, and that his dad had been clinically butchered there.

Behind the abattoir was a narrow lane that led to Forth Banks, and down to the quayside. During the week the quay was usually occupied by ships crews, dockers, job hunters, and the idle sightseers.

But on a Saturday morning, the City Road end of the quay was taken over by the second-hand merchants hawking their cast-off clothing and footwear; and is still in vogue to this day. On a Sunday morning when I was a lad, and right up into my late twenties, the scene on the quayside was unique as far as open-air markets go. Not only were all the usual commercial household traders present that frequent such markets, along with the ice cream merchants and tea stalls; there were characters present, occupying all the vacant spaces between the stalls, whose behaviour, intentionally or otherwise, made the weekly visit a most humorous and worthwhile occasion. There were quack doctors, who claimed to be able to eradicate almost every complaint that one could suffer from; with the exception of course, poverty; two well known individuals who took turns in securing one another up in strait-jackets, and chains, then escaping from them, after the collection; one regular attendant who chewed and swallowed glass, razor blades, and even Woodbines much to the disgust of those in the audience who obviously were gasping for a smoke and could not afford to; last but not least, there were a number of individuals, some of whom were shabbily dressed and sad looking, who were attempting to sell racing tips, which they professed to have obtained personally the day previous from either Lord Derby, Lord Ascot, Lord Roseberry, or some other celebrity high up in the racing world. I often wondered why these men, especially the shabby and sad looking ones did not back those certainties themselves, then perhaps be in a position to purchase a suit, a pair of shoes, and a cap.

Naturally of course the tipsters like all the traders on the quay were out after earning a few bob, and not to amuse their audience; but the pathetic appearance of some of them, coupled with their extravagant claims, inevitably provided the usual odd heckler with many a punch-line, that soon had the audience in stitches.

The town centre was out of bounds to me, being forbidden to wander there by my father; though I often safely managed to ignore his warnings at times. For instance on many a Saturday evening I was in the Grainger market near closing time, which was quite an experience; and many a raw black pudding and huge piece of tripe, did I devour then, given to me by some kindly butcher. Row upon row of butchers, all attempting to dispose of the remaining steaks, joints, chops, sausage and black puddings, due to lack of proper refrigeration on their premises.

All shouting together: "Hear-hear, luk, Missus, luk, Sir, this way, hinny, a big joint of brisket, pound of sausage, two chops, an'a whole black puddin', th'lot for five bob —. Wait a minute, hinny — divint gan away — it's yours for four bob."

I would stand and wonder why on earth there were so many butchers, grocers, fruit shops, and general dealers, all practically on top of one another? Surely it was competition gone mad. However, if one possessed a sense of humour, it was entertaining to stand aside witnessing these trade people becoming excited, agitated, but somehow, never did they display anger, or become rude.

Just a few yards away from the Grainger market, was the wholesale fruit and vegetable market, and containing as many characters as Dickens himself could have scrambled up at any one time. I well remember one chap, an odd job man, who hung around the market making himself available to any beck and call. He would haul a barrow of merchandise from the market to any distance, up hill, and down hill; all for a few coppers; yet he never complained of his lot. All he ever expected was a bite to eat, and a kip in the Sally Army; and this was all he ever did get! "Blessed are the meek, for they shall inherit bugger all."

My first vivid recollection before the age of five, concerns my first day at Cannon Street infants school; and being escorted there by my sister Kitty; who was two years older than me, and quite a serious child for her age. On the way to school I witnessed my first funeral; the pallbearers were busy placing the coffin into the horse driven glass hearse; there was another coach behind for the chief mourners, while the remainder of the congregation were beginning to assemble behind it to walk to the cemetery. The dismal sight depressed further my already low spirits, for having to attend school was certainly not my choice.

Being expected to do as I was told at home, held me in good standing that first morning in the classroom. I was given a picture book to look at, and told to sit quite still, and I did just that. But by midday, rebellious feelings were beginning to develop within me. When the lunchtime bell sounded, my first thoughts were solely on escaping from the building as swift as my legs would carry me, with the firm view of never returning. Before I could act on this impulse, my sister entered the room, and gaining my teacher's permission, she escorted me to the school dining hall; where to my surprise and delight I was provided with a free appetising lunch. On learning afterwards, that I was to have such a free repast every day at school, I somehow overcame my reluctance to be caged-in, and educated.

Home was a two room flat, and by now there were eight of us living in them. On the same landing as us, lived a family of four, occupying the two front rooms; downstairs lived a family of five; all of us sharing the same backyard, toilet, and wash house; living space was at a premium. On weekends if the weather happened to be inclement, then underneath one of the two double beds, was my favourite playground, indeed my only playground. So as time progressed, I began to look forward to going to school to get away from communal living, and the irritation it created.

Saturday was Busker's Day. In Benwell there was the choice of listening to an accordionist playing and singing in the back lane; or climb the backstairs and down the front stairs into the street to witness the antics of the'One Man Band', who was everyone's favourite, and a well known character. This old boy travelled the length and breadth of Newcastle and Gateshead; including all the pit villages, month in and month out, in all weathers; and he was getting on in years then.

One particular Saturday afternoon, a man and a woman on a motor cycle entered the street; parking the machine against a lamp post, they both took off their coats and goggles. He then opened up a large saddle bag that was secured to the machine and brought out a portable gramophone, on to which he placed a large record and set it playing They then began dancing, holding each other very close; suddenly, without any warning, and showing no signs of temper, the man threw the woman away from him, and she fell to the ground. But no sooner down, than she jumped up again and gracefully threw herself into his arms. A little more dancing clinging together, then once more she was thrown to the ground, apparently dragged along by her hair, kicked, so it seemed, then up she sprang again and into his arms. I enquired of our next door neighbour. "What on earth was going on, and whether someone ought not to go to the Police, before this bloke decided to injure her." It amazed me no end, why a man should bring his wife; or mistress; or girl friend, to a strange district on the back of a motor cycle, and then to the rhythm of dance music, proceed to knock hell out of her. The neighbour patted me on the head, grinning awhile: "It's the Passion-elle, son, a French dance," said he, obviously enjoying the performance. Somehow the entertainment repulsed me, for I could not get it out of my mind, that the man was ill-treating his partner. Mind you, I could quite understand some of the men present, enjoying the spectacle, for they themselves threw their wives about without any pretence of dancing with them; and that unfortunately included my old man.

Saturday was also ticket-man day. From nine o'clock in the morning, and on throughout the afternoon, these hopeful money-collectors came from all directions, and representing almost every firm in the city that gave credit. "Knock-knock." "Money all spent, cum back next week hinny."

It is true that Wyatt Earp kept Dodge City clear of Outlaws; and even sent a few of them on a one-way journey to Boot Hill; it is equally true, that many of us in our neighbourhood sent a fair number of ticket-men on to the scrap-heap; if not with the colt, then certainly with a weapon just as effective — nervous debility!

The family living in the front two rooms on our landing, consisted of the parents, and two young boys; they were an extremely nice family. But the youngest boy possessed one of the most monotonous high pitched voices ever to be heard. When their ticket man came every Saturday, about lunch time, he would knock loud on the street door, and call out up the stairs "Provident". The youngest boy would be sent out on to the landing, and he would shout out in this high-pitched tone, "Me muffer not in you," And the

10

poor little fat ticket man would fiercely retort, "Your mother is in."

"Me muffer not in, you."

"Your mother is in-so don't give me that."

"Me muffer not in, you."

This usually went on for about ten minutes without a pause, both participants becoming irritable; until finally the man went away in distress muttering to himself. At one time the agent on one of those weeks he was not being paid, would climb the stairs and attempt to argue it out with the lad: "Don't tell lies to me, your mother is in." "Me muffer not in, you."

Then one particular Saturday my father had gone out to him and gave him ten seconds to vanish; the fat man disappeared in four.

Now one good turn deserves another; so when our own ticket-man, from another credit company, called in the afternoon, my brother John would be sent out on the landing to deal with him; and for some peculiar reason of his, he rather enjoyed these weekly skirmishes when there was nothing in the kitty, to pay the agent. Out he would go on to the landing and in a loud clear voice, declare. "Me muthers oot, me da's oot, an'we've got nee money, so there."

"That's what yer told me last week, think I'm a fool or some-thin'," would be the usual retort from our frustrated money-collector.

Unsympathetically my brother would reply. "We've niver got any money in wore hoose, Mister, yer better cal' next week."

This battle like its earlier counterpart, would also rage on for a few minutes; often to the amusement of a gang of kids attracted by the sound of the argument. Then once, our next door neighbour came out on to the landing, pretending to he in a furious mood: "Stop bloody arguin' with th'kid, if yer want t'argue, al come doon th'stairs with yer." And off went our ticket-man in a hurry!

What a hopeless way to make a living, even during times of depression and lack of work. However, as the business firms they represented never went bankrupt during this period of heavy unemployment, then thankfully no one was apparently any the worse for it; certainly not the debtors.

Weekend was also pitch-and-toss time in the back lane; needless to say this pastime, could often end in a punch-up; which I suppose was another way of entertaining the bystanders, who could not afford to join in the gambling. Men fighting in back lanes over the issue of two-headed pennies, or playing cards concealed up someone's sleeve, was bad enough; but when two women got to grips in the lane, over the issue of Johnny hashing Jimmy, then the spectacle could be really primitive: and the sight always held me spellbound with excitement, and fear. A fight in one lane was swiftly reported in the next: and perhaps in the next also by some lad rushing down the lane calling in a very excited voice: "Cum iveryone — cum quick, there's a fight in oor lane they're morderin' one another." And sure enough the kids and teenagers, with the odd adult, would follow the crier, as though he was the "Benwell Pied Piper".

When I became of age to attend junior classes, I was transferred to Elswick Road school. The first morning, I was again escorted by my sister Kitty, who impressed upon me not to attempt to cross the terrace until I came to the school crossing, where a Policeman was always present during school hours on traffic duty.

We set off from home about eight thirty, and a glance in both directions along the terrace satisfied me of the necessity for such precaution; commerce was on the move! Apart from the tramcars clanging, and rattling along the tram-lines appearing like huge fairground shuggyboats there were horse driven vans in great profusion, along with the odd horse and cart of the tatter (scrap merchant)and the coal merchant. The horse's of Jenning's bakery; and of Ringtons tea company, bore the appearance of well groomed race horses; and they could move, no tramcar could ever hope to keep pace with them. In my opinion they were the finest commercial beasts ever to be harnessed to a delivery van. The brewery horses were large beautiful majestic creatures, and their presence, strength, and grace, would have made any farmer green with envy. As regarding the droppings, of these hard-working four-footed creatures; no road sweeper ever had cause to stoop, for the local allotment holders were on continuous patrol with their home-made bogies.

After a couple of weeks or so, I was trusted to go to school on my own, mainly for two reasons; my sister could not keep pace with me; and secondly, my father discovered in me the capabilities of being a unique errand boy; I always appeared to be able to get the goods. My sister being the oldest, was always sent any errand that entailed going down on to the terrace. However as the grocery shops had fixed times of opening it invariably meant she had to bustle in order to get to school on time. One morning she revolted and told my father to send me on to the terrace, claiming I was a fast runner, and would still be able to get to school before the bell rang.

The very next morning, my father got me out of bed at seven prompt. Ten minutes later I was quietly going down the front stairs with a carrier bag and threepence. Up the street I ran, along Gill Street, which ran parallel to the terrace, and into Beech Street; Jennings the bakery occupied the whole of one side of it. As I entered the main entrance I observed the delivery men harnessing and coupling their horses to the vans in preparation for the days rounds.

In the bakery itself. I was approached by a giant of a man; whom I learned later was the foreman baker. He glanced down at me in a most quizzical fashion, as though amazed at my sudden appearance.

"What can I do for you nipper?" said he. Tilting my head back I looked up to him. a most engaging smile upon my face: "Hav'yer got threepenneth of old breed, mister, please?"

He continued gazing down at me for a few seconds; I sensed somehow that my mission was in the balance: "I hope you've got sum, mister," I added, "because when I get back yem, I've got t'gan on th'terrace for bacon pieces, an'if I get sum we'll al'have bacon sandwiches for breakfast."

He ran a large thick finger across his top lip as though intending to conceal a smile: "Alright, hinny, give me yer bag I'll see what I've got for you."

When he returned from the large bread bin that appeared to house the previous days bread, I observed that my bag was bulging. Handing over the threepence, I thanked him about half a dozen times. Arriving back home my father praised me, and declared it was the best threepenneth we ever had scored for; and there and then, appointed me as chief message runner, as though he was doing me a favour. After a mug of weak tea, and a slice of bread, I was then sent down on to the terrace in search of a penneth of bacon pieces. I made direct to the Co-op, knowing my mother did her main shopping there. But I soon discovered that as far as the manager and staff of the Co-op were concerned, I was not going to receive any co-operation from them in my search for bacon pieces. Indeed through time, I was to learn that neither my wit or my most engaging smile were to create any impression upon the co-op; whether my quest was for bacon pieces, cracked eggs, spare ribs, broken biscuits, or even firewood; so much for their brand of co-operation, thought I.

Returning back along the terrace I called into Duncan's stores; and was immediately supplied with a fair sized package of bacon pieces, and also rewarded with a beautiful smile from the young assistant; whom I took to be about sixteen years old. For two whole years she continued to keep for me a regular supply of all the above mentioned commodities that I failed to obtain at the co-op. Then sadly she departed; whether to take up another position, or to be married, I never did learn.

I was eight years old now, and the most remarkable thing about me, apart from my swiftness; was my appetite; and due to it, I always rose in the morning raving with hunger, and went to bed at night in the same plight. I could never get my hunger satisfied, even on those mornings when I was rewarded with an extra slice of bread and marge, for my being successful in my daily search for cheap sources of provisions. I would go to school and sit in the classroom oblivious of my teacher rambling on, perhaps about the exploits of King Arthur; or the wonders of the Steam engine: my thoughts were inevitably on the free dinner I would receive at lunch time. If there were second helpings to be had I could always be relied upon to devour my first, in time to score for the second. Yet when I came out of the dining room, I was still capable of eating more had the opportunity arose. I don't wish to create the impression that I was a glutton; but I was aware then, as I am now, that all young animals, human, or otherwise, are capable of eating and digesting large amounts of food; and like many more in my circumstances at the time, rations were very limited at home, and also in the school dining room; unless one was fortunate enough to be chosen to be a dining hall monitor.

One day coming out of the dining hall, a class-mate of mine told me to accompany him along Elswick Road to a small factory workshop opposite Elswick Park.

Before we entered, he instructed me on what we were after. Inside, the men were sitting by their various benches, reading newspapers, and drinking tea. We strolled from bench to bench asking the men if they had any bait left over. Our mission was a great success, and in the park opposite we sat on the grass stuffing ourselves royally. What we had left we concealed under our jerseys for afternoon break time.

Also in our classroom, were two brothers, orphans, whose orphanage incidentally, was directly opposite the factory where we had collected the bait. Although these two lads were always better dressed than myself, and well shod, they also must have been restricted in the home, as regarding rations. At break time I shared out my remaining sandwiches with them; and continued to do so every day afterwards.

However, one or two more hungry lads got wind of our bait trips, and soon my friend Roy, and I, had to face brisk competition. Thereafter, speed was the most essential factor, and as Roy and I, were both swift runners, it inevitably led to a few skirmishes with the other competitors who arrived too late. So it was agreed by one and all, that whoever reached the factory first and scored, would share out with the rest of us; the result obviously was back to lean times again.

On a rare occasion if I had a penny on a Saturday, and providing I did not spend it on a lucky bag, or a quarter of liquorice allsorts, or on bruised fruit, I was able to escape from my usual surroundings for a couple of hours by going to the Adelaide Cinema on the terrace; or to the Majestic, or the Grand, both situated

17

on Condercum Road. These last two cinemas on a Saturday, employed a chap for a few coppers, who would shout his lungs hoarse urging the approaching children to spend their pennies in the particular cinema that employed them. The man employed by the Majestic shouting, "Don't go into th-loppy Grand, its full of fleas, cum in here, we've got '*Fatty an' Skinny*' on, *Buck Jones*, an' *Mickey Mouse*." The chap employed by the Grand, would be retorting, "Cum in here, its Charlie Chaplin, Harold Lloyd, an' Tim McCoy." The majority of us were frustrated before we had finally made up our minds. But the Majestic, which was the better equipped cinema, and the easiest to dodge-in if one was skint, was often the one to fill up first.

Monday was poss-tub day, down our lane. Considering most of the men were unemployed at the time, the womenfolk had muscles that even Samson himself would have envied; as fit as my father was, any odd time he felt like washing his own shirt before the official wash-day, he would ask my mother to wring it out for him, with her bare hands, rather than going downstairs to use the wringer in the backyard wash house. On a Monday weather providing, street traders had to beware; none of them were allowed, or able to get down the lane with their horse and carts, or barrows, for the lane was occupied from top to bottom with everyone's weekly wash. The kipper man, milk woman, fruitman, or coalman, were obliged to remain at either end of the lane, or use the front street to hawk their wares whether they liked it or not.

I remember one woman in particular; no names mentioned, who was six foot tall, and weighed about fourteen stone, one of the strongest women I've ever met; she was the only woman I knew of who was never ill-treated once by her husband, it was usually the other way round. One particular Monday morning, during the school holidays as I was playing marbles in the lane with some of the other lads, a coalman came into the lane, a stranger he was; in order to progress down the lane he began lifting up the sheets of this big woman, and wrapping them over the clothes-line; one of the lads playing marbles at the time, excused himself, ran into the big woman's backyard calling out, "Missus — th'coalman is pullin' doon yer clean sheets with his hackey han's."

Out into the lane came this towering Amazon. She grabbed hold of this bewildered coalman, and practically pushed him and his horse and cart loaded with coal, back up the lane chastising him meanwhile in her wonderful bass voice, that sounded like a distant roll of thunder. Both man, and horse, appeared afterwards to be in a state of shock.

CHAPTER
TWO

My First Visit to the Pawnshop

Like most men in the neighbourhood, my father was unemployed; but he would not hang around street corners; and with eight of us to feed he could not afford to do so. Therefore from a Monday to Friday, he went tatting, for rags and woollens, and lumber. Of course he had to be secretive about it, for if the labour exchange were to learn of his expeditions he would have his dole suspended.

One Monday, after been out all day with a barrow, he returned home failing to earn one penny piece. Next morning after I had returned from seeking the old bread and bacon pieces; he parcelled up his navy blue suit, the only suit he possessed, and instructed me to go to a particular pawnshop. "Here, son, ask for ten shillings on that suit; now make sure you go to the man, not his wife; she has the eyesight of an eagle. Do you understand son?"

"Yes, da," I replied. This was my first trip ever to a pawnshop; down the front stairs I went into the street and set off at a gallop! Whenever I was sent a message, which by this time in my life I considered too frequent, I always pretended to be a cowboy, for by kidding myself thus, it took some of the monotony out of the task, and I saw to it that each of my favourite Western heroes got a turn each. Starting on a Monday morning going for old bread, it was the turn of Tom Mix; going for bacon pieces or cracked eggs, it was the turn of Ken Maynard; Tim McCoy he usually got the late night run to the fishshop; at that late hour I was often given enough chips and batter for twopence to feed all of us; Tom Tyler, took over at school time; and now at last I was able to fit in Buck Jones to the pawnshop trail.

On arriving in the next street where the pawnshop was situated, I gave a good look around to see whether any of the local lads were about, if anyone going to my school had spotted me, the fact would have been broadcast all over the school yard. The coast was clear so I slipped round to the back entrance. Standing in the backyard, was a smartly dressed middle-aged woman; she appeared nervous, as well she might, for she did not look the type who frequented pawnshops.

"Are you going in there, son?" She smiled feebly at me

"Yes, Missus, what can I do for yer?" replied I, a little puzzled, for I assumed what she was after yet apart from her handbag she was empty handed.

"I wonder whether you could take something in for me — I'm not accustomed to these places."

She no doubt thought I was, and although it was my first visit too, I reckoned between the two of us, the chances were no doubt that I would be the one who would become the seasoned visitor.

"What do yer want taken in Missus?" said I, getting to the point, for it was getting close to school time. She opened her handbag took out a jewellery box about six inches long and placed it into my hand.

"Could you please ask for six pounds for that son, in the name of Jenson."

She was a posh talker, and very smart; I wondered if she had any children?

"Where d'yer live, Missus?"

She looked at me in alarm, her face becoming flushed with fright I think: "Oh don't worry about that, son, I shall wait here for you."

"Yer have t'give an address, Missus, otherwise they tak'nowt in."

She hesitated a little.

"152 Bentinck Road, son," she finally replied.

I entered the back entrance of the pawnshop, and quietly glanced into the first cubicle. Madam, was at the counter talking with another woman in the next cubicle, she gave me a sharp glance as I closed the door. Moving along the passage I entered the end cubicle, the Governor was standing behind the counter facing me; the door snapped behind me with a clash, and he began staring at me in an irritable manner, as though my arrival there was solely with the intent of annoying him.

"Well, what can I do for you?" said he rather abruptly.

I pushed the parcel over the counter towards him. "A soot for ten bob please, Callaghan is the name ——" "I know your address," said he interrupting me. and implying. "I hear it often enough in this place."

He untied the parcel and began to examine the suit. I deliberately shoved the jewellery box over to him, hoping to distract him from my father's suit, which I knew could not bear too close an examination. His eyes lit up at the sight of the box, and he subjected me to a short severe scrutiny, as though he had found me out in some conspiracy or other.

"Six pound's on that for Missus Jenson, 152 Bentinck Road, please," said I ignoring him staring at me.

"You live quite a distance from Bentinck Road," said he.

I observed his wife, who was still leaning on the counter facing number two cubicle, paying attention to her husband's remarks.

"Ah nar Bentinck Road is a lang way from my street," replied I indignantly, assuming the basis of his suspicions. "Missus Jenson is standin' ootside in th'backyard — its not my fault if she's afraid t'cum in th'panshop."

He blinked his eyelids repeatedly for a few seconds, as though answering me in a form of morse code; then once more cast his attention on to the suit.

"Seven shillings," he remarked disdainfully.

I was neither disappointed nor annoyed, for I knew well that my father only expected to be given seven shillings on it; indeed he realised also, that the first time

23

Madam got her eyes on his suit it would be pensioned off! Making out the ticket, he handed it over along with the money; then opened the jewellery box and brought out a necklace and a pretty brooch. At the sight of the jewellery, his wife, who was still displaying an interest into her husband's manoeuvres, excused herself to the woman in cubicle two, and approached her husband. In what I took to be a rude gesture, she took the pieces of jewellery out of her husband's hands without saying a word, and producing an eyeglass from out of her apron pocket fitted it to one of her eyes and examined the necklace and brooch under a bright desk lamp. Looking obviously satisfied as to their value, she nodded to her husband and returned him the jewellery. Gracing me with a stern look, she returned to her former position at the other end of the counter.

"Six pounds for Jenson," said her husband, sounding like an auctioneer; and most likely wishing to reassert himself, after the interference from her, for he had sheepishly returned his own eyeglass to his coat pocket without ever using it.

Somehow I was becoming to like the man; and much later on in our acquaintance, I began identifying his abrupt manners as a kind of reaction in opposition to his wife's possible overbearing attitude towards him in public. On receiving the money and pawn ticket for the jewellery, I went back out into the backyard. Mrs. Jenson appeared in a state of agitation; perhaps the poor woman had thought I had foolishly scarpered out of the front entrance. I handed her the money and ticket and her features relaxed, she even smiled in a composed manner. Opening her bag she took out her purse, put in the notes and the pawn ticket, then rewarded me to my surprise with a two shilling piece; I wondered whether she had taken leave of her senses; never since I had become the target of all the errand shy women in the neighbourhood, had I visualised that it was possible to earn so much money for such little effort, and it was only on account of her fashionable attire, and posh voice, that encouraged me to accept the coin; I know I embarrassed her with my sincere gratitude. On arriving home I gave my father his pledge money; and discreetly slipped the two shilling piece to my mother, explaining how I earned it; and was rewarded with twopence, which to me was quite a fortune.

It was raining heavy when I came out of the school dining hall; shrugging my shoulders in dismay I set off at a trot down the bank towards Scotswood Road. My father had told me that morning to pay a visit during my lunch time to my Aunt Dolly, who had a second-hand clothing store, and enquire whether she had a pair of shoes or boots to fit me. The downpour was making my worn-out canvass shoes feel twice as heavy on my feet; yet I still wondered whether I would be better off if I had a good solid pair of leather shoes on my feet, or a raincoat to protect my shoulders.

I had no sooner entered the shop, when I was followed in by a young couple, who broke off what had sounded like a running argument. The lady sported a carnation in the lapel of her shabby raincoat; her young man did not have a flower in his coat, but he did have a safety-pin conspicuously secured in the seat of his trousers. Around his eyes could be detected faint black shadows, the obvious trade-marks of either a coal miner, or a sweep. He remarked that he was after a decent cheap suit, costing no more than ten bob. My Aunt soon learned from his young woman that they were intending to be married at the registry office later that afternoon; and from him, she discovered he had been in full employment for the past five months down the local colliery. On the strength of his apparent prospects, he was out to prove the age old belief, that two could live as cheaply as one, a fallacy, in which no doubt he would be fully supported by the family, relatives, employers, and in time possibly the Labour Exchange.

My own luck was out, despite a thorough search of the shop by my Aunt. Outside on Scotswood Road while waiting for a pause in the traffic so as I could cross the road, I was accosted by a tall, fairly well dressed man, who appeared to be on a pub crawl. He gazed down sympathetically upon my deplorable footwear. Suddenly, on the spur of the moment, he enquired what size shoes I took? "Size eight, Mister," replied I a little puzzled. "Stand back in that doorway out of the rain a little while and I'll see what I can do for you," said he.

Now quite a number of shops in my young days, practised the habit of displaying their merchandise outside their premises unattended. A few yards back along the road from where I was sheltering at the time, was a shoe shop, the staff of which had apparently decided to ignore the state of the weather, and had left boots and shoes hanging up outside secured by twine. This unsolicited intending benefactor of mine walked directly up to this display of footwear, and extracting a jack-knife from his trouser pocket began examining the soles of the various children's boots, obviously searching for size eight.

Amazing though it may seem, either no one observed him, or they simply decided to ignore his self-help scheme. He cut down two boots, and unmolested returned and offered them to me. Despite his kind intentions, I shook my head determinedly: "No thanks mister, me da would give me a gud hidin' if I took them home."

I learned later of course, that shopkeepers were not all that simple or obliging; they only displayed odd specimens of footwear outside their premises, and never in pairs. Had the big man had his wits about him he would surely have known this; but, such was the gravity of the beer in those days, so I'm told.

Next morning the rain was still belting down, as I set off to the bakery. Arriving there I brought out my carrier bag from out my trouser pocket.

"Gud mornin', sur, hav'yer threepenneth of owld breed please?"

He turned round from the mobile trolley which he was busy loading up for the vans.

"Hellow, nipper, old bread, yis I think I can manage that for a little workin' lad like yerself. Mind, yer wet through, hinny."

The large drops of tear shaped rain were streaming down my face into my eyes and mouth.

"Is rain gud for yer hair, mister?" I enquired of him.

He laughed then looking down at my feet at the dilapidated canvas shoes, the laughter vanished from his face: "I don't think its too gud for yer feet nipper. What size shoes do yer tak', son?"

I cast my eyes down to his own feet, my jove his cast-offs would be of no use to me, by God he had large feet.

"Size eight," replied I, not very hopeful. He shook his head in dismay. "Hm-pity, my lad tak's size ten."

I was not surprised to learn that. Taking my carrier bag off me and the money, he went over to the left-over bin and filled my bag with loaves. As I turned to leave the warm dry building, he called me back.

"Wait a minute, hinny," said he.

Going over towards the ovens, he came back with a hot mince pie and handed it to me.

"Here, nipper, stuff yerself with that hot pie."

I thanked him kindly, and off I ran through the storm munching the hot pie that was rapidly cooling, with the aid of rainwater. Climbing our front stairs I entered the room, the one we described as the living room; in reality, it was a bit of everything: kitchen, bedroom, and bathroom in the winter when it was too cold to be washed in the poss-tub in the backyard. Everyone excepting my younger sister were up and about; the scene resembled a hive of productivity; some washing, some dressing, two of my brothers drying on the same towel, for everything had to be shared in our house; crockery, footwear, socks, beds, the lot!

After I returned from the terrace with the bacon pieces, my father cut, and shaped cardboard soles and slipped them inside my shoes. Long before I got to school the cardboard soles were saturated. As young as I was I knew the whole exercise was pointless; however my father would not brook any criticism from any of his offspring.

When I arrived at the main school crossing, the Policeman on traffic duty was busy as usual dealing with the flow of tramcars, motors, and horse-and-carts. In between his directing of the traffic, I observed to my dismay that he appeared to be giving me more than my deserved share of scrutiny. I allowed my thoughts to run backward through my memory-closet, attempting to pinpoint what I may have been guilty of lately that he personally was aware of. Finally he waved a group of us over; when I was level with him, he placed a large hand on to my shoulder.

"What's your name, son?" said he, in his most official manner. I looked up at him.

"Av dun nowt, sir, nowt at all," replied I, determined to deny anything.

He took a break from his point duty, and escorted me over to the school gates, meanwhile taking out his notebook and pencil. Once again he repeated the question, and I told him.

"Where do you live?" he inquired next.

I'm being pinched, thought I, though completely in the dark as to why.

"What size shoes shoes do you take, son?"

I gave a deep sigh of relief, for I thought I was going to be charged for setting my buck-up to fist waving tramcar drivers, who had spotted me riding on the outside steps. When he dismissed me, I ran into school hoping to beat the bell; for punctuality was one of my earnest trademarks.

When I arrived home that afternoon from school at four thirty, I learned a Policeman had called in the afternoon and left me a new pair of leather boots; the first ever to my knowledge, for any footwear or garment that came our way was inevitably second-hand.

For some odd reason, the Policeman had overlooked laces; and it took trips to two local shops, and finally the pawnshop before I could obtain some free twine, which I had to blacken over with boot polish.

CHAPTER
THREE

A Visit from
My Granny

By the time I was ten years old, I considered myself as local messenger boy; I also had a Saturday job with a greengrocer on the terrace. I was old enough to realise that every penny I could earn would be an important contribution towards the family budget. It was while I was employed in the fruit shop, that I got the idea of selling firewood. Mrs. Race, the proprietor of the shop, who was a kindly soul, always gave me a wooden box after completing my delivery round. This I took home for our own use; but on receiving two boxes one Saturday, I chopped them up and sold half of the firewood for sixpence. I immediately realised the possibilities of being able to earn three times or more, by selling firewood on a Saturday as I earned on my delivery round. When I confided in Mrs. Race, giving her the reason for deciding to pack in my Saturday job, she understood; and to her credit, she continued at times to supply me with the raw material for my new venture, in the shape of wooden boxes.

One evening on returning from school, I was informed by Ginger, a big strapping lad who was two or three years older than myself; that there was a demolition job in progress nearby, and an abundance of firewood to be had. With my tea rations in one hand, and my axe secured in a sack in the other, I accompanied him down on the far side of the terrace. The doomed large house within its own grounds had recently been occupied by a local midwife and her two children.

It was a sad sight to me to witness one of Benwell's well known land-marks being demolished blow by blow. The house and grounds had always spelt mystery to me; it was the kind of residence I would have loved to have been reared in. Never again would I be able to raid its orchards; in its large grounds were to rise blocks of Sutton Dwelling flats. However, business as always in this world of ours, appears to take precedence over sentiment; so Ginger and myself grabbed what wood we could, and he broke it into suitable lengths with his huge hands, I chopped them into sticks. It was about nine o'clock before we had completed our last sale of firewood. I took a sack full home, and as I sat on the fender watching some of the firewood blaze, I felt as though I too was guilty of having taken part in destroying such a fine old house and estate.

Despite my father's painstaking precautions on his tatting rounds, the thing he dreaded of all — that of being detected by official snoopers — occurred, and as a result his dole was temporary suspended.

Rations at home in the best of times were slim enough without this catastrophe: one of the many cuts to be applied to the family budget was in having to make redundant the gas meter so, when darkness fell in the evenings, life had to continue in the dull glow of the fire.

One morning during this period my father informed me I was to stay away from school for the day, and assist my mother by keeping an eye on my young sister Mary. So after a scant breakfast the three of us set out towards the offices of the local Board of Guardians, where my mother intended to apply for a relief ticket.

The Parish guardians operated from a large house surrounded by a spacious garden, which had once been a private residence. The scene in the waiting room was too drab and depressing to even attempt to describe. We sat down, my sister on my mother's knee; and within seconds another woman engaged my mother in conversation. One may think their own personal troubles are chronic, until they look around, and listen to the pathetic chatter going on about them. The lady talking to my mother, had her husband ill in bed, there were only two blankets on the bed, no surplus coats available in order to supplement the scant bedding, and no food in the house.

The woman next to her had three young children with her, and although it was twenty minutes past nine in the morning, the four of them had not eaten since teatime the night previous. Various unhappy looking children were crying out through restlessness, and no doubt misery; and the Usher was doing his utmost to encourage their parents to keep them quiet.

When it came to my mother's turn I placed my sister's hand in my own, and quietly followed her into the interviewing room.

Behind the table sat two men and a woman, smartly dressed, and obviously better fed than any of the claimants having to appear in front of them. They took turns in asking my mother questions. They were undoubtedly experts at stripping one of their meek dignity; nothing appeared from their point of view, to be too sacred; their thrusts, and probing, were anything but delicate. During the relentless questioning, each of them in turn, glanced at me and my sister, as though we were a couple of objectionable specimens. The verdict of these adjudicators was unanimous; no relief until they had sent an official to visit us, and do more probing.

"Well, hinny," remarked my mother, once we were outside the grounds of the inquisition, "I am going to Blaydon to see my brother."

I offered to go with her and keep an eye on my sister. She had the carfare only to Scotswood Bridge; from there we crossed over the bridge and walked into Blaydon, and it proved a long weary journey with having my sister along. Arriving in Blaydon, we called at my uncle's house; I took it to be a mansion, and could only think that my uncle must be a very rich man. He was out, and my Aunt never asked us in. So we walked around Blaydon and finally came across him in one of his shops. He gave my sister and me a banana, and placed us in charge of one of the shop assistants, then he took my mother through to an office at the back of the shop. On their way out. I observed him slip to my mother what appeared to be a pound note.

I thought he would have volunteered to drive us part of the way back in his car, but no such luck, and having just missed the country bus, we retraced our steps back to the trams of Scotswood.

"Tom, it's your turn!" My father was calling on me from the backyard. I was the last one for the poss-tub, which was used for bathing every Sunday, weather providing. Although it was early October, the sun was shining and it was pretty mild. Downstairs I descended in my birthday suit, and my father lifted me into the tub. Though we were always hard-up, water and carbolic soap were always available in liberal supply.

I was aware at the time, that my father had no coppers to buy himself some Woodbines so he was in a hell-ava mood, and I was determined not to cry out if soap suds seeped into my eyes, for under the circumstances, he would not hesitate to ram the block of soap between my teeth; which would only serve to amuse Ginger, who was sitting on the back wall, at the request of my father, in order to keep the other local kids away from the scene until the bathing session was over. We lads, always suffered this public indignity on a Sunday on account of having no bathroom; my sisters were bathed upstairs in front of the fire. On this particular Sunday, my father was really going to work on us, as after dinner we were all going to attend

Sunday school whether we were in a religious fervour or not, though on a purely voluntary basis of course.

Although my mother was religious, my father, was completely indifferent as to who created the world, or for what purpose. So one may inquire, "why was my father laundering us extra careful, and offering encouragement to us to attend Sunday school?"

Well, it was only ten weeks to Christmas, and all the churches in the area always provided a free Christmas feed on Christmas morning, for those children-in-need, who attended Sunday school for a reasonable period before Xmas. Our routine, which was carried out also by other kids in the area, simply meant that we went to a different church each year, regardless of denomination; we were not biased; and they all provided about the same in treats, a meat square, a bag of cakes, fruit, a paper hat, and as much strong tea as one could drink. Indeed all the charity tea I ever consumed when a child was nearly as potent as Newcastle Brown Ale.

Of course we could have avoided the necessity of having to change Sunday school year by year, and inevitably a trek as the more local churches had to be considered out of bounds, lest the Sunday school teachers caught on to our game, simply by attending one Sunday school all the year round. However, there were two reasons which discouraged us; first, the lack of our wardrobe; secondly, all of us were apparently five-day week advocates; nothing but compulsion would have driven us to Sunday classes fifty-two weeks a year.

Until my father had enlisted the aid of Ginger, who possessed hands like pan shovels and was very capable in using them, the regular Sunday backyard scrub in the poss-tub, had been a source of amusement to most of the other kids in the lane. As soon as my father had lit the fire in the boiler house to heat the bath water, the smoke and sparks shooting up the chimney from the firewood, always attracted the attention of one or two lads who would then run the length of the lane calling on the other kids: "Hey, cum an' see th'Callaghan's gettin' bathed in th'backyard, they've got nowt on." And within minutes about a dozen or more lads, all shapes and sizes would be sitting on top of the back-yard wall overlooking our backyard, taking the rise out of my old man, and each of us in particular.

I usually went to chapel with either my brother Arthur, or John. When we came out of Sunday school we always did the christening rounds! There was always a regular delivery of new babies in the area, and Sunday was a favourite time for the proud parents to have them christened. It was a custom for them to hand out to some passing individual the "christening", which was a small package usually containing a portion of cake, and a scone with a silver threepence or sixpence, wrapped up in a small piece of tissue paper inside it. In practice, the happy couple gave it to the first kiddy they met near the church, and as my brother and I patrolled all the local churches, our chances were always high.

One Sunday after chapel, and after doing the christening rounds, my brother John and myself set off for home. As we were climbing the stairs an unusual smell assailed our nostrils, and it was coming from our living room, we obviously had company for someone must be smoking a pipe. We entered the room, and the first thing we observed was a halo of smoke rising above the old rocking chair; someone was sitting on the chair wearing a cap, and a thick black shawl draped round the shoulders; I took the visitor to be that of an old man.

My father was standing behind the chair and he encouraged us to come forward and greet our grandmother; and sure enough, the owner of the cap, shawl, and clay pipe, was a very old woman. She kissed my brother John, put him aside, then turned her attention on me.

"So this is the laddie who's called after me poor Thomas," said she in a fairly robust voice, for such an old lady. "Come here, me boy, and kiss your Granny."

Her son Thomas had been killed in Flanders in 1916. She placed her arms around me; and at that moment I thought I would much rather be kissed by my Sunday school teacher, who was young, pretty, and who did not smoke a clay pipe; I could almost taste the foul tobacco as she kissed me on the lips.

I was amazed to learn she was ninety years old; and wondered how she had travelled alone from Bishop Auckland, the day previous.

My mother was busy baking at the time, and my granny took it upon herself to engage the children's attention, with the view I suppose of keeping us out of our mother's way, which was quite a problem in such cramped quarters. For such an old lady she appeared to possess a remarkably clear memory. First she began relating on her own childhood back in Dublin, then afterwards on her early experiences on leaving home and coming to England to work in private service. She was a most interesting narrator, and as we discovered, a unique story teller. She told us what life had been like in her young days, working as a servant in the big houses; some of her reminiscence's were gruesome, in as much they set me shuddering, to learn how shocking some employers could treat their servant girls. At the time, I thought my life was all work; running endless messages, attending school, selling firewood in my spare time, instead of playing at cowboys; but young as I was then, I instantly realised that I had no cause to complain after listening to her remarks. Seventeen hours a day was her usual norm as a young servant; her work had been hard and tedious, and the wages, and free-time, paltry.

Leaving home at eighteen, and after travelling to England from Dublin, worn out; her employer, instead of feeding her, and packing her off to bed in order to recuperate from the journey, immediately set her to work, and it was near midnight before she was dismissed from the scullery. She soon learned, that as far as the maid below stairs was concerned, very little compassion, understanding, and good manners, would be directed towards her.

This was the domestic atmosphere below stairs, that my grandmother began to experience in the early 1860s.

I have since learned that such attitudes towards servants die very hard, for during the 1950s, I too worked as a servant in the houses of the upper-middle class, and in the mansions of the rich, and discovered that some of them appear to assume that servants are akin to robots, requiring but little sustenance and rest.

My grandmother professed to have believed in the "Little People"; but I now think her claims were solely to amaze and amuse a group of young children who were sitting at her feet absolutely spellbound. I remember even now so clearly, listening to her that Sunday afternoon in 1934, relating her versions on the origins of the "Crock of Gold"; and "The Blarney Stone". I remember also, two particular Leprechauns who were prominent in both of the tales. One was nicknamed "Red Nose", on account of his glowing beacon, gained, so she told us, by his over indulgence in Poteen (illicitly distilled whisky); the other little fellow was nicknamed "Long-Stride", on account of him being the swiftest little man she ever did meet. It appeared these two celebrities were once invited to a banquet which was being held by the little people, to honour the first visit to Ireland of the Welsh Queen of the Fairies; and every Leprechaun present was expected to tell a story.

Long Stride was the first to enter the circle. "My Majesty, friends, my story's about the origin of the Crock of Gold. One night many years ago, I was at a gathering up in Antrim, along with Red Nose. Having just completed a most delicious meal, we began on the grog. Now in a nearby pasture, there was a Fenian encampment: none other so we learned later, than that of Red O'Brien himself. We had heard men earlier bawling out with their fiery rebel songs. However, later that evening, so preoccupied were we with our music and singing, that a huge shaggy-faced stranger was among us before we realised it; he appeared to be just as surprised to see us, as we were to see him — he stood and gaped at us for awhile; and I assure you all, his fiery red beard and hair, and his blazing eyes, were a sight to disturb anyone. Not wishing trouble, we invited him to a drink, and were reassured when he sat down peacefully. Obviously our drinking vessels were like thimbles in the hands of this huge creature, so after a while, and more in a display of impatience, than with intending bad manners, he cast aside the small mug he had been provided with, and lifting up the main brew container, he began drinking, and continued until he drank the contents, the greedy divil he was! I must here add, that there was something extra special about our large brew container, it was made of solid gold and of a most beautiful design, made of course by that most illustrious of all craftsmen Nimble Fingers.

"The stranger was about to replace the container down, when by the glare of our fire, his large eyes began admiring the artistry of the dish. When he realised the vessel was of solid gold, he visibly shook with excitement.

"'This dish is magnificent,' said he, 'and I Red O'Brien say so.'

"Suddenly, without saying another word he jumped to his feet and ran off in the direction of his camp, still holding on to the valuable dish; and twenty of us chasing him. Of course when he reached the safety of his camp, we were hopelessly outnumbered.

"Two weeks, Red Nose and myself, followed O'Brien and his band of Fenians, and finally arrived at his stronghold. One night when we did manage to break in when all inside were asleep, and search around thoroughly, all we could discover were two leather bags of newly minted gold coins; after a close examination of the hoard, we realised in disgust, that the heathen had coined them by melting down the priceless brew container. To further increase our discomfort, I had the misfortune to accidentally step right on to the head of a huge sleeping hound, which apparently was lying outside the bedroom door of O'Brien. We ran out of the house, over the fields, through streams, and into some woods, where we managed to lose those who were pursuing us. However we kept running for we could still hear the powerful voice of O'Brien, in the distance, calling out, 'Bring back me gold, you undersized villains.'

"After a while we arrived at a small village, and as luck would have it, one of the inhabitants, who was looking out of his window, instead of being in bed where he ought to have been at such an early hour, spotted us; out he came and began chasing us, meanwhile calling out to all and sundry, to follow in the chase. Being so worn out by now we realised that unless we could distract this lot, long enough to enable us to get out of sight we were sure to be caught and dispossessed of all the gold.

"'Let us throw a couple of these gold coins towards them,' said Red Nose, 'for that will sure set them fighting among themselves.'

"At the end of the village street we suddenly halted, threw a couple of coins in their direction, and instantly they set about each other like a pack of wolves, and so we managed to make our escape.

"However, from that day onward, word spread throughout Ireland, that every Leprechaun had a crock of gold buried somewhere, and you only had to capture one of them in order to become rich."

With a cup of tea in her hand, and her pipe, now resting on the hob, my grandmother now related her version on the "Origin of the Blarney stone".

However I shall tell it only briefly. I may add, that my father, who was sitting on the edge of the bed behind us, was interesting himself in the stories, with complete amusement all over his face.

The story was about how Red Nose, was being pestered by a colleen who desired to become his wife, and of course cure him of his drinking habits. But he resisted all her wiles and refused to submit. One day while he was sitting by a stream, repairing his brogues, she happened to pass by, and after a few words of greeting sat down by his side. Curiously for one wishing to cure him of his drinking habits, she offered him a drink of wine from a bottle she had in her basket. Unwittingly he accepted, and within minutes of downing the wine became inflicted with a most terrible thirst. Suddenly with a uncontrollable urge he literally threw himself into the stream, and began attempting to quench the thirst. But the more he drank the more the terrible thirst increased its powers upon him.

"What have you done to me?" cried out Red Nose, in disgust and fear.

"I have ministered to you a potion of 'Constant thirst' and you will continue to be afflicted by having to drink water, night and day non stop, for two long years, you heartless wretch," she screamed out in between cries of anger and fits of devilish laughter.

"You know I hate water, you witch," called out Red Nose, in great distress. But off she took herself, never to return.

Night came along but no relief did he get, he was exhausted, yet compelled by the over-powering thirst to remain by the stream.

Just before noon on the following day, Long-Stride came on the scene. On learning from his friend what his troubles were, he announced he would depart instantly in order to seek the aid of the great Leprechaun magician, Sean McGinty.

Apparently after inflicting the curse upon Red Nose, the colleen herself, had went direct to the magician, and had concocted some tale of how Red Nose had rejected her loving advances, and ill-treated her. The wise man, in order to pacify her, and thus keep up his good relations with the fair sex, promised her, "That as Red Nose, had acted towards her as though he were made of stone, then so shall he become stone, until the end of time!" He directed her to visit the stronghold of the tyrants, McCarthy's, on a given day, and at noon on that same day to kiss a certain stone situated high-up on the battlements, which would be marked with an X. On doing so, she would be both appeased and revenged; not to mention being rewarded with the rich gift of eloquence, the likes of which has never been heard of. And thereafter, anyone who kisses the same stone shall be likewise rewarded. People shall come from far and wide to seek this gift. It shall become known as the Blarney Stone; out of evil shall come forth good.

The magician refused to explain further; however, she left his presence apparently quite satisfied with her visit.

It was the wise man's intention of directing Red Nose, to proceed to the castle on the same day; but to arrive one hour earlier at eleven o'clock in the morning; and when he kissed the stone, by magic he would be automatically incarcerated into the stone.

But when Long Stride, appeared in front of the magician and related what the same colleen had inflicted upon Red Nose, he was so infuriated with her deceit, that not only did he cure Red Nose of the infliction, but he arranged that Red Nose should turn up at the castle on the given day, not at eleven the fateful hour, but two hours later!

So Red Nose arrived in the village of which later was to become known as Blarney; climbed up the castle wall, and at precisely one hour after noon, pressed his lips to this particular stone, and to his amazement he heard the voice of the colleen from within it, cursing him yet again with his heartlessness and treachery. After recovering from his surprise. Red Nose, in his rich Dublin accent, began giving her a good dressing down, and enjoying every minute of it.

Unknown to himself however, one of the sentries on the battlement was discreetly observing the whole peculiar scene; and thus became convinced on hearing such eloquence coming from such a little man, that the particular stone he had witnessed Red Nose to kiss, must be possessed with magical properties.

Thus through the witness of one lonely soldier, did the tale of the "Blarney stone" become to be told all over Ireland.

I don't suppose I have quoted the stories word for word, as my grandmother told them, but the basic contents of them are identical.

After tea, she sent me a message to the top corner shop for an ounce of twist tobacco and a box of matches. Out of the change of the half-crown, she gave a penny each to my brothers and sisters; I was also presented with a glass toy which she took out of her bag. The scene inside the toy depicted a small village street with an old couple walking along it; when you shook the toy a snow storm was created. She remained that night with us; it is amazing how many can squeeze into a double bed.

That visit from my maternal grandmother was her first to us, and unfortunately, was her last, for she returned to Bishop Auckland. She died nearly five years later.

Not long after granny departed for home; we moved house down one of the streets that led from off the other side of the terrace; and consequently we moved to another school also. Our final school was South Benwell, a huge three storey grim fortress looking building: it was overcrowded; completely devoid of comfort for both pupils and staff; the heating during the winter months was totally inadequate due to the main defects of the building; and the sanitary arrangements were I suppose what was to be expected in the playground of a monstrosity that ought to have been demolished on the demise of Queen Victoria. However despite the criticisms I make of such an unbeautiful citadel, I have to confess, that in South Benwell school, it was my pleasure to become aquainted with some of the most dedicated teachers of that profession: Mr. Cowie; Mr. Smart; Mr. Dixon; Mr. Poole; men, who but for the stranglehold being exercised on the educational expenditure at the time, would have been teaching in the classrooms of the schools of higher education; and not through lack of opportunities, having to remain content teaching a purposeless curcurriculum, in return for a miserable salary, in an elementary school.

In the junior classroom of a Miss Nash, I believe I spent some of the happiest of my schooldays. She was a young, pretty, dark haired, trim looking woman. I became infatuated with the whole of her character from the beginning; she was kind and gentle; and despite the contrary opinions of one or two of her colleagues in the junior school, she was in my opinion, a capable teacher, educational wise.

Looking back to those far-off days, I sincerely believe that it was her obvious kindness and gentleness, that resulted in her downfall as far as teaching at South Benwell school was concerned. For on the eve of my elevation to the senior school, she was dismissed for not being able to control the small rowdy element in the class! Some children unfortunately, so unused are they to having kindness and gentleness bestowed upon them, look upon such virtues, as a display of weakness, and thus they react to such beneficence, in a most provocative manner.

The pupil who sat next to me in the junior class, sharing the same desk, was a girl called Anne. I have forgotten her surname; not that I would mention it if I could remember; but she lived above Laws Stores, on Benwell Terrace. Although I was only ten when we first met, and introduced to each other by Miss Nash, our teacher, I developed, a crush on her, which lasted from then right up till I reached my late teens. Unfortunately for me, acute shyness prevented me ever making any attempt to question, and discover whether she entertained any romantic notions towards me.

The very last time I set eyes upon Anne, was during the war, when she was on leave from the Wrens. I walked her home; at least I assumed she was living there, it was in a house attached to a church on Two Ball Lonnen. Still I could not muster sufficient courage to ask her for a date.

However, the romance which was born, and which developed in perhaps my mind only, was nevertheless my very first, and I still think, my sweetest.

CHAPTER
FOUR

Family Wardrobe

After breakfast one Saturday morning, my mother inquired of me whether I would like to go to my Aunt Dolly, and watch the shop, time she went to Paddy's Market? I replied eagerly in the affirmative.

Most of the second-hand shops on that road to Blaydon, dealt practically in everything; from cycles, prams, pots and pans, clothing, footwear, pictures, etc. But not my aunt; apart from the pictures on the wall of the shop, she dealt exclusively in clothing, footwear, and handbags: furthermore, most of her stock was collected by her from the homes of the posh people in Newcastle. As far as she was concerned, every item she displayed for sale on her premises were fit to be placed in anyone's wardrobe; all at give-away prices.

Down the bank I went, and waited beside the tram stop. When it arrived it was nearly full of women, all apparently on their way down to the Grainger market, to do their weekend shopping; the car resembled comfort wise, one of the two-tier cattle wagons that I often witnessed progressing along Scotswood Road on its way to either the cattle market, or the slaughterhouse. However the fact that the tram was about loaded, suited me ideally, I considered the poor Conductor would be busy enough collecting all the other fares, without my troubling him; so I sat on the outside step of the car unobserved by him. Each stop we came to, I simply stood aside and allowed those passengers wishing to alight, or board, to do so, then jump on to the outside steps of the car as it moved off again; keeping my eyes peeled for any signs of an approaching conductor; or any tram Inspector, or Policeman, on the road.

Mind you I was not the only lad in the neighbourhood who practised this stunt; and as regarding the loss of revenue it entailed the corporation as a result, I don't suppose any of us bothered: We kids had nowt, so what was good enough for us, was surely good enough for them.

I should add, that as a lad, I was a fervent supporter of "free public transport", it would have solved in my humble opinion, all the worries of the transport department, and of the travelling public, especially mine.

I arrived at the shop about eight. Davey, who sold the Evening Chronicle, six nights a week outside the Marble Bar, in the town, was busy assisting my aunt to load up the handcart which was just outside the shop door, with merchandise which she was taking to Paddy's market, on the Quayside. Davey looked a sight as usual. My aunt, often attempted to tidy him up; providing him with a suit and an overcoat; but the little chap was one of those unfortunate creatures, whom you could give the Moss Brothers treatment to on a

Monday, and within two days later, he would resemble a worn-out dosser. He had the habit of sleeping in his clothes, whether it was in the Salvation Army hostel; Donnelly's lodging house; or at the back of my aunt's shop, which he often did when funds were low; and funds were invariably low, for only two concerns profited by his selling of the evening papers, the proprietors, and the Marble bar.

I had no sooner entered the shop when one of the quayside racing tipsters entered, enquiring whether there were any hard hats in stock.

"I'm after a nice cheap dut, Dolly, if you have one dear," said he, in his usual professional, swaggering tone, as though he believed himself to be a race-horse owner, and not a tipster who was so hard-up, he had often to write out his tips on the inside of empty cigarette packets.

Busy as she was in her preparations for the market, my aunt, did not like the idea of an unsatisfied customer leaving her shop, and so she began searching high and low for a dut to fit the racing gent. Not one could she find; mind you there were one or two trilbys available which were his fit, but he would not hear tell of such headgear; for a man of his calling, it had to be a dut. My aunt appeared to be towards the end of her tether:

"Wait there a moment, bonny lad," and off she went into the living quarters.

The obviously inquisitive tipster cast a scornful glance on to poor little Davey, who was standing

51

nearby, doing his utmost to be as inconspicuous as possible.

"Who's that scarecrow standin' there?" inquired the tipster, addressing me.

"That's Davey," replied I, "He's gannin't'help me Aunty, with th' barrow on t'th'quayside."

"Him help her, he's not big enough to reach th'barrow," said he in an insolent manner.

Davey, who wouldn't harm a fly; began edging himself out of sight into the shadows, towards the rear of the shop. Aunt Dolly returned with a hard hat; and I instantly guessed, that when my Uncle Charley next looked into his wardrobe, he was going to discover one of his duts, was missing.

"Here, bonny lad, try this one for size," said she.

It fitted him perfectly, yet he even had the cheek to haggle over the price. I was confident, if my uncle had of got out of bed and entered the shop in search of his hat at that moment, this tipster would have had to run a sight lot faster than some of the horses he often tipped as certainties.

When he left the shop; she handed me a list of prices: "There, bonny lad, if anyone wants to buy something just look at th'list, al'th'prices are on it —. Now there's sausages an'eggs in th'kitchen, get your Uncle to cook some for you," She put her coat on, secured a scarf round her head, and was about to leave the shop when I reminded her about the dut! "What shall I tell me Uncle if he begins lookin' in here for his dut?"

"Tell him he lost it last night, when he got himself well-served along th'road," replied she, quite unconcerned.

Off she went, Davey pulling the barrow, and herself pushing it from the rear-full of beans was my Aunt Dolly.

I always got sixpence for helping out in the shop, plus two shillings for my mother, providing my aunt had a successful morning on the Quay. Last but not least, being in the shop on my own, gave me the opportunity to play at dressing-up. In long trousers, and a trilby, I pretended to be Tom Mix, and I would stand in front of the full sized mirror practising the quick-draw with an imaginary six-shooter; then afterwards, I would replace the trilby with a dut, and pretend to be Charlie Chaplin. I was suddenly interrupted in my masquerade, by the entrance of a buxom, rosy-cheeked woman. I took off the trilby in which I had been acting a cowboy part; and greeted her.

"Hello, hinny, where's yer Aunt?" "She's gone t'Paddy's market," I replied.

At that precise moment, my uncle Charley entered the shop from the direction of the kitchen, dressed in trousers, braces, vest and slippers.

"Where's that aunt of yours, Thomas?" said he, appearing, and sounding cross with himself.

"Gone t'Paddy's market, uncle," said I.

"Then what to hell has she done with my other dut?" He came right up to where I stood, before he set eyes upon the buxom woman. Blinking his eyes once or twice, he finally got her in focus; and he gave her an approving scrutiny. "Excuse me, hinny, I didn't see you just then." He once more turned his attention on to me, peering at me suspiciously as though I was in the conspiracy regarding his missing dut: "Well, me dut, where's it?"

"Me aunt says you lost it last night when yer were well served."

Poor uncle Charley, he was really exasperated. "Me lost it —? She's flogged it, that's what she's done, the cow." He went over to admire his photo which was framed and hung up next to a print of "Uncle Toby". After giving the buxom woman another approving glance, he retreated off into the living quarters, cursing to himself.

"So that's Dolly's man is it? He's a queer bugger," remarked the customer. Moving over to the mobile clothing racks, she began searching among the ladies coats. "I'm after a cheap dark coat, son. You see, I bury my father on Monday, so I must look respectable. Did yer aunt sell yer uncle's dut?"

I observed she was carefully examining the lining of each coat on the rack, that appeared to take her fancy. "I think me uncle lost his hat last neet," said I, not intending to offer any information on the question. She took off her own coat hung it on the end of the rack, and tried on a red coat and began admiring herself in front of the long mirror. I wondered whether she was colour blind? "I thought yer wanted a black coat Missus — for the funeral?"

"I like this coat, son, I could place a black armband on it for a few days —. How much is it? I'll bet it's every penny of seven an'six." "All big coats on that rack are ten bob, Missus; they're nearly new, an' they al'come from the posh people."

She rewarded me with a cold defiant look. "Well, there's no posh people in this neighbourhood hinny," replied she. "I think you've made a mistake, ten shillin's is a week's wage to some people; perhaps yer mean seven an'six? I know Dolly wouldn't ask a penny above that sum." I sat down on the old trunk impatiently; wishing she had never come in the shop, interrupting my cowboy performance, to haggle about red coats, and black armbands.

"You see, hinny, I didn't get much insurance money; my father looked so strong an'healthy, none of us expected him to go sudden, without givin'us some warnin'." She placed all the other coats she had been looking over, back on to the rack, but decided to keep the red coat on. Then with her back to me, she opened her purse, I heard the rustle of paper, then she turned around and pushed a ten shilling note into my hand: "There, give that t'yer aunt, it's a lot of money for a coat."

Wearing the red coat, and with what I took to be her own over her arm, she walked briskly out of the shop.

I moved over to the rack intending to tidy it up, and to my amazement, observed she had cunningly left her old coat behind and taken a good dark coat in its place; two bargains for the price of one. I ran outside, but she had vanished. I began to hope my aunt was perhaps unfamiliar with stock-taking.

Back inside the shop I took up the discarded shabby coat and threw it on the floor at the back of the shop, deciding it would do for little Davey to kip on sometime.

My uncle came into the shop wearing his good black suit. "Black soots yer, uncle, better than broon." Of course I was soft-soaping him, for I wished to get him in a good mood, a cooking mood. He ignored me and moved over to the far wall to admire his photo again. Turning round, he looked me straight in the eyes, "I may as well get used to wearing black, Thomas, for that aunt of yours will soon be attending a funeral, her own, the cow that she is."

Uncle Charley, never curtailed his language in front of no one, not even clergymen.

"I'm hungry, uncle, how aboot some eggs an'sausages?" By now he had moved towards the full sized mirror, and was gazing into it. Truthfully, when my uncle was sober, and keeping a straight face, he wasn't a bad looking chap.

"Christ, Thomas, I don't wish to start cooking in this suit. You go and cook for both of us, I'll watch the shop."

My aunt had consistently warned me never to leave my uncle alone in the shop, for if he sold anything he always pocketed the cash: however, I had no alternative my stomach would not tolerate to be neglected when there was food to be got.

"Don't be long, son, I've got to go to work!" said he.

"Work," thought I. "Him sitting in a pub along the road taking bets and drinking Bass, until three o'clock.

If he had to fiddle like my old man, pulling a barrow around all day hawking for rags and scrap, he wouldn't have time to make faces in the mirror."

Half an hour later I returned to the shop, and my uncle departed for his breakfast.

He returned just in time to witness the local Parish Priest enter the shop with a collecting tin in one hand.

"Oh Christ, I thought I would be away before he came," remarked my uncle, to me. Of course the Priest heard him for he was not one to whisper. "Tell him your aunt's out," said he, retreating back into the quarters.

"My aunty is out," said I to the priest, "An'me uncle is in a bad mood because he lost his hat last neet."

And my uncle, who apparently was concealing himself behind the kitchen door, called out: "Don't tell lies, Thomas, I didn't lose me hat, your aunt flogged it."

The priest shrugged his shoulders and smiled, "Not to worry, son, I'll see your aunt this afternoon, and perhaps I might come across your uncle in the bar."

When he left, my uncle came out of hiding, muttering furiously to himself. He went outside on to the pavement to observe where the priest was heading for, returning he made a critical remark: "I'll bar him, he ought to keep out of pubs, he never puts a bet on."

A little later my uncle left the shop too.

About eleven o'clock, a young lady entered; she was perhaps twenty years of age, good looking, and very smart despite her poor attire. She certainly appeared a different kettle-of-fish than the buxom woman who believed in having two coats for the price of one.

She inquired as to whether there were any costumes in the shop? I pointed out the particular rack, and then sat down on the old trunk. Somehow, I sensed she was pretending to herself that she was shopping in one of the big stores up town, in place of a second-hand shop; though mind you, I must insist again, my Aunt Dolly's, wardrobe cast-offs, were definitely good value. She selected a costume and held it up to her figure to judge the fit, I suppose. I felt she would look good in blue, and told her so. She smiled, apparently pleased that I was taking an interest.

"Could I try it on, do you think?" said she, rather timidly, I thought. "Of course," said I, and directed her to the rear of the shop just in case anyone was to enter. As regarding my own presence, I felt sure she was not concerned; I was only eleven years old; nevertheless, I found it an interesting spectacle witnessing her change. Having judged her slim figure with her frock on, I was amazed when she removed it, at the size of her shapely thighs.

Dressed in the costume she admired herself in front of the mirror, it suited her perfectly. She turned to face me with a look of anxiety. "How much is this one, son?"

I consulted my price list. "Twelve shillin's, miss." Disappointment took over from anxiety. She opened her handbag and brought out her purse. "I've only got ten shillings."

As I remained silent, she slowly walked back into the shadows again, intending to change into her frock. I knew from personal experience that my aunt would allow no unsatisfied customer to leave her premises if a reasonable reduction in the selling price was required to clinch a deal; so whether my taking it upon myself to follow her example would result in my total banishment from the shop in future, I made my decision. "Could yer afford ten bob, Miss?"

She eagerly returned to where I was sitting. "Are you sure you won't get wrong?"

"I don't think so, me aunt's gud-hearted, she'll let me off," replied I, thrilled at the obvious pleasure I was giving her. Handing me the money, she rolled up her frock and placed it under her arm, leaving the shop quite happy.

I had just made a cup of tea for myself, when a quaint looking individual entered the shop with an overcoat over his arm. His eyes were glazed as though he was in some sort of trance. He held up the coat towards me as though desiring me to examine it. "It's a gud coat eh? It used to be my brother's. Luk at th'inside label — 'Burton's', they don't sell rubbish do they?"

"And me Aunt doesn't buy rubbish either," thought I, looking sadly at the dilapidated garment which appeared and smelt, as though it had recently been used as bedding for some mangy dog. I gathered what his mission was, but even if the coat had of been in a remarkably good condition. I was in no position to bargain with him, that was solely aunt's prerogative, and I told him so; and also informed him where my aunt was. "Why don't yer go doon t'Paddy's market," I said, "Your sure t'get rid of it doon there." Knowing full well of course that not even a dosser in a drunken state, would entertain his offer.

"Two an'six, an'its yours," said he, completely ignoring my explanations. "I can't buy anythin', Mister," I replied, "Yer better gan t' Paddy's market."

"Balls Paddy's market," said he, beginning to concentrate his attention on to my mug of tea. "How aboot a drop of tea then, an'a bit of scran, am clammin?"

As young as I was, I realised by the man's odd appearance and behaviour, that he was a dosser. I knew there was time for me to provide him with some tea and a sandwich without any fear of being surprised by the return of my aunt, or her daughter, for I did not expect either of them back before one thirty, or two o'clock. What concerned me was leaving him alone in the shop, he could very well vanish with one or two garments as soon as I was out of sight; however, feeling sorry for the man I decided to take a chance.

When I returned with a mug of tea and a cheese sandwich, I discovered him gazing at the pictures on the wall; and I sighed with relief! Many years later, while I was on the "Road", I learned that among the various categories of homeless men I came across, the "dosser", who remains permanently in one town or city of his choice, and sleeps rough, is invariably one of the most trustworthy and harmless creatures among them.

After completing his repast, he thanked me, and left stating he was going into the town in order to sell his coat. No doubt the only possessions the poor man had were his obvious illusions; for his belief that he would be able to sell such a distasteful garment to anyone, could not be attributed to any firm conviction or hope.

The pictures that decorated the walls of the shop, were mainly of Victorian character portraits, and Newcastle city scenes. They were priced at between seven and sixpence, and ten shillings each; today, those same prints would each realise a fair sum; yet none of the locals who entered the shop to explore, ever gave them a second glance.

About one o'clock, a tall middle aged gentleman entered; by his dress, and apparent style, I wondered whether he may have been one of the Theatre Royal actors. The trilby he wore, was as big and wide as that worn by Tim McCoy, another western hero of mine. Everything about his appearance expressed affluence and sheer contentment with life. He instantly designed to ignore me, and the various racks of clothing; but strolled leisurely towards the nearest display of pictures upon the wall. Out of his vest pocket he produced a pair of golden coloured pince-nez, affixing them on to his nose, he first glanced at the photo of my Uncle Charley, and began chuckling to himself; which he could afford to do so with my uncle being out of the way. Then slowly he examined each picture with meticulous care; mumbling to himself awhile, such phrases as, "How delightful; extraordinary; how sweet."

Completing his tour, he appeared quite satisfied with himself, and in a mood to acknowledge my presence. He lifted his hat slightly, as a token of greeting. "Now then, my young man, are you by chance the proprietor of this establishment or perhaps an assistant. Which?" I pondered over the word proprietor, not quite sure what it meant, but I did sense business. "If yer want t'buy anythin', Sir, yer pay me, 'cause me aunt is at Paddy's market."

He appeared very interested at the information.

"Tell me," said he, "Where does this Irishman hold his market, where your aunt has gone to?"

"What Irishman?" replied I, rather baffled at his question.

"But did you not just say your aunt was at Paddy's market," retorted he, in such a tone that seemed to imply I was having a quiz game at his expense.

"That's th'name of the market, Mister; people go there t'buy second-hand clothes."

He rubbed his hands together as though he was going through the motion of washing them. "Ah — now then, we are getting somewhere. Tell me, are there any pictures for sale there?"

"I don't know," I replied, "Av niver been there."

"Ah, I see. Well then, what do you think of those pictures up on the wall here?"

"I think they're gud, Mister; me da says that my aunt is givin'them away at those prices." I felt certain my remark did not go down too well with him.

"Oh, does he?" said the big man. "Well, son, have you got a phone on the premises?"

"There's nee telephone here, Mister; there's a box over the'road," said I, wishing he would go into it and remain there.

"Right, but first of all, follow me round time I take those pictures down, then I shall total the cost."

After we had placed them down carefully on top of the trunk, he went outside to phone a taxi. When it arrived. I assisted him in taking out the pictures, and after paying me, he gave me a shilling for myself; I immediately changed my opinion of him when I felt that coin safely tucked away in my sock; my mother would get that. Before he left the shop, he rewarded my uncle's photo with a final glance and a soft chuckle: and said, more or less to himself, "What an unusual face that man has." Aunt Dolly and Davey returned shortly after his departure. I gathered both of them had sunk a jar or two, on the way back from the quay. After we unloaded the barrow of the unsold merchandise, Davey went off to return the barrow, and proceed to his newspaper pitch.

"Aunt Dolly, I let a young woman have that blue costume for ten bob, does it matter?" said I.

She only shrugged her shoulders, and replied, "Never mind, bonny lad, none of us will ever be rich, th'times are too hard."

I observed her gazing at the bare walls: "An a queer dressed man came in an'bought al'the pictures. He seemed to be interested in me uncle's photo."

"Then you ought to have sold him that as well," remarked she, smiling to herself.

"Uncle Charley is goin't'bury yer aunty, that's what he said before he went to the pub."

"I'll see him out of this world first, bonny lad, don't worry." (And she did.)

CHAPTER
FIVE

I Become a Newsboy

When I entered the back lane, the usual crowd were present playing pitch-and-toss. There was a time when I got the job of "toot"; that is the one who remains at the bottom of the lane keeping an eye open for any sight of a Policeman who may suddenly decide to follow his feet off the terrace and peer into the lane; but unfortunately running messages kept me occupied now on a Saturday afternoon.

Two men were arguing with each other: "Hey, just watch it noo, am tellin'yer, keep yer bloody han's doon — an'stop barrin'th'pennies!" called out Big Bob, to the man whose turn it was to toss.

"It's ma turn. I av'a reet t'bar them if I wish," replied the tosser.

"Not ivery bloody time yer toss," retorted the big man, displaying his over-sized fists practically under his opponent's nose.

I often wondered why they allowed this particular man who was at the moment tossing the coins, to play pitch-and-toss, for if he was losing, which was often, then he would resort to any practice to prolong his agony. I supposed the fact that he was always losing, was the only reason they allowed him to participate.

Despite the business-like warning from the big fellah, he again handled the pennies on their downward fall; and was bundled out of the game, and finally out of sight, when he refused to pipe down.

Soon the game came to an end; it was eleven o'clock, the corner pubs on the terrace would be withdrawing their bolts; those who had won the toss, would enter the pubs; they who had lost would stand outside on the corner in the hope of being invited inside later.

I sat down in the lane with the other lads for one of our popular buskers had just arrived. He began playing his accordion, and singing — "Marta", aided by a funnel shaped gadget which was affixed so as it remained close to his mouth. I think this chap styled himself on Arthur Tracey the street singer; and on my reckoning, he was very good; indeed I could not remember as a lad ever witnessing and listening to a rotten busker, they were all good artists.

After his turn was over he came round collecting, quite a number of the onlookers placed a halfpenny or a penny if they could afford it into his cloth bag. After he departed from the lane, the next merchant to appear, was a robust looking woman pushing a bogie containing three milk churns in it. Picking up a hand bell from out of the bogie, she rang it loud and clear. When she ceased ringing the bell, she called out in a powerful voice, "Skimmed milk, skimmed milk, three-halfpence a pint, cum an'get it."

All the grown-ups had gone back inside at the departure of the busker, but one of the women soon reappeared at her back door, and in a voice nearly every bit as robust as that of the milk vendor, called out to her boy, who was sitting by my side discussing the wedding "hoy-oots". "Harry, cum an'get th'jug son, an'git a pint of milk for yer mother." Harry jumped up as though he had suddenly been catapulted from a strong bow. "Cummin', ma," and off he disappeared into the house, to return instantly with the jug.

Soon I heard the familiar sound of my father's voice. I too jumped to attention, as though a firework had been set alight from under me. Parents in my neighbourhood, when I was a lad, expected immediate results whenever they sang out their clarion call, to their offspring. It was of no use kidding we were hard of hearing, or too tired at that particular moment, for they had swift and effective treatment for any such ailments.

My father stood at the back-door in his trousers and vest; a jug in his hand. "Tom, here, a pint of milk and no drinking of it, and three-halfpence change."

After all had been served with their wants, off went the milk woman in the opposite direction to that of the busker. I often wondered whether these merchants had prior knowledge of each other's movements, for two of them never appeared together in the same lane!

Though, I do remember an exception; it had occurred two years previous; I was nine at the time, and on my summer holidays. A fish merchant, hauling a handcart, entered the lane from the bottom end at the precise moment another merchant, also with a handcart, appeared at the top of the lane, selling oranges. The orange vendor, possessed a voice as robust as any opera tenor, and he was only a small man. The hawker selling kippers, resembled someone who could have possessed an operatic tenor voice, yet his vocal capabilities were almost ineffective as far as hawking was concerned. The powerful voice of the little man selling oranges, was obviously annoying the kipper merchant; so much so, that he began walking up the lane towards the orange man in a most threatening manner: "There's nee bugger can hear me with yer bloody shoutin', yer little waster," called out the kipper man, who was red in the face with temper, "I'll ram every bloody orange doon yer gullet."

The fish hawker, hadn't the sense to realise that all he need do, was to hold his breath, allow the little man to do all the shouting, which would inevitably bring out into the lane intending customers, and the curious; who on observing the kipper man and wishing to do some business with him, would naturally do so. But no, the frustrated fish vendor, by now waving his huge fists about in the air, continued his advance up towards his believed tormentor; meanwhile the little man was continuing selling his oranges and taking not the least bit of notice of the approaching antagonist. By now at least three cats, taking advantage of no one in attendance over the fish cart, were on board it, sniffing with delight.

One of the kids called out to the fish man: "Mister, the moggies are eatin'yer kippers," The big man halted in his tracks, swinging himself around, and grasping the situation he ran down towards his barrow; amazingly enough, only one of the cats had the wit to make off with a free meal. The kipper man decided our lane was not worth patronising. and as he prepared to leave, he called up the lane in a voice as strong as he could muster, "You up there with yer bruised fruit, don't dare follow me t'th'next lane, yer little scarecrow, or I'll throttle yer." And off he went, cursing the orange vendor, the cats, and everyone else in sight.

However, to get back to the previous scene; soon after the milk woman had departed, my brother John came into the lane and called me into lunch. It was half past twelve, and games were over for the day, I had other plans for after dinner. As I went through the backyard, the downstairs neighbour was standing by his door arguing with his wife who was in the scullery, because she would not loan him twopence for a packet of Woodbines.

I found my brothers and sisters already eating their chips and bread; my father sat near the window looking out on the yard, amusing himself at the continuation of the Woodbine appeal going on downstairs. After lunch my mother prepared to go shopping on the terrace; after arranging with her the time and place where I would meet her to assist in carrying it back, I went down the backstairs, down the lane on to the terrace and ran all the way to Benwell Parish Church, in time for the afternoon weddings.

There were about ten other lads around the church gates, and as usual Ginger, was in charge; a fact which no one disputed if they desired to remain in the vicinity. The bells began to peal for a minute or two, then the first happy couple of the afternoon session came out of the church, least they were smiling; and to judge by their prosperous rigouts, neither groom or bride, could have ever set eyes upon the inside of a Labour Exchange, or Parish Guardian office cap in hand, begging for a food ticket; unless the poor buggers had borrowed the clothes.

The whole wedding group numbered eight, and the photographer was in his glory, as he may well have been for they were desiring to be photographed from all angles. "That's gannin't'cost a pretty penny, al'them photo's they're havin," remarked this regular spectator, who for some reason or other never failed to put in an appearance at the church gates whenever there were weddings or funerals taking place. Finally the bride, bridegroom, and best man, got into the first car that was alongside the gates Ginger firmly ordered the majority of the kids to congregate round the second car; he knew, and I knew, that if the best man did not fling out a handful of coins out of the car window as the vehicle pulled away, then there was little or no chance of the occupants of the second or remaining cars doing so. However, we always felt it necessary to impress both the groom and his best man, that we kids were not present at the ceremony solely to admire the scenery with any undue sentiment, for most of us present could have told anyone of the happy couples a thing or two about marriage bliss; we were after money for various reasons, and the only way to remind them was to call out continuously— "hoy-oot, hoy-oot". And as the first car pulled away from the kerb, that is exactly what the best man and the groom did. No one was more swifter than myself, not even Ginger; and the instant those coins were thrown out, both of us were sprawled out over the tramlines after grabbing as many of the falling coins as it was possible. A man passing by at the time could not resist the temptation and attempted to join in the scramble, but Ginger, although only thirteen at the time, was a big heavy lad, and he used his superior weight to discourage him, and so the poor man gave up the attempt. An approaching tramcar, its warning bell clanging away and sounding more like a fire engine, made not a penneth of difference to us, we continued the struggle. The tram driver had to jam on his brakes and drop his safety guard at the front of the car. Opening his front window he stuck his head out. cursing us and shaking a fist: "Get back to yer back lanes, you lot of savages," he called out.

We rose up out of his path, and Ginger, in turn began cursing him: "Move this load of scrap-iron oot th'way, av'got my livin't'mak'as well." With a final curse the driver continued his journey.

I believed he might report the incident to the first Bobby he came across on the terrace; so I decided to keep one sharp eye on all the best men: and another open eye scanning for the possible approach of the local Coppers. My father had forbidden me to come to these wedding hoy-oots, so it would not do for me to have myself booked by the law.

The church bells pealed out once more and the second wedding party came out of the church. The bride was dressed completely in blue, even her hair was blue. The bridegroom, and the best man, who appeared to be brothers, were undeniably scowling at each other. I wondered to myself, "Whether the bride had chosen the wrong brother? Or whether one of the brothers had picked the wrong bride?" Be it as it may, but the poor photographer got very little opportunity to spend much time under the black cloth that appeared to envelope his tripod camera; two snaps and he got his dismissal.

The four guests who made up the wedding group, were none the less smiling heartily to one another, and appeared to be enjoying the obvious discomfort of the other three. Ginger and myself, grasped the situation, and we told the other lads to congregate round the bride's car stating that it was their turn to have the best car. The first vehicle bearing the bride, groom, and best man, pulled away swiftly, as though the driver had been urged to attempt to lose the four cheery looking guests who were then climbing into the second car; not a nickel did they throw out. The second car was not long in following, and surprisingly enough, the four exuberant occupants, as though displaying their disapproval of the meanness of the occupants in the first car, each, threw out a handful of coins. The falling pennies from heaven, was too much a temptation to ignore, and two or three of the poor fag starved men standing round, literally threw themselves on to the tram-lines as though intent on suicide; and the following scramble was none too gentle. It was perfect training for any young healthy lad who anticipated someday becoming either a rugby player, or an all-in wrestler.

Just as I got back on to my feet, I caught sight of the shining helmet, as the owner of it, all six foot of him, appeared on the corner, beside the Grand cinema. He had just witnessed the aftermath of the scuffle, which also had held up an approaching tramcar. As soon as he made a move in our direction I tugged at Ginger's coat sleeve: "Hey, Ginger, th'Copper's comin' — am off!" Over the tram lines I fled, on to the quarry with Ginger, close behind me.

We made our way to the wreck of a saloon car, which had been dumped over the hill from above. Climbing inside, myself behind the driving wheel. I suggested we play at speed cops: but not him. I could never remember him playing any childish game, such as cowboys, yet he was only thirteen: his pastimes were gambling and smoking; so all his spare time had to be devoted to cash raising. He pulled out his Woodbines, and lit one: but one of his good points was he would never encourage another minor to smoke, on the contrary he would discourageage them. But towards any old gaffer, who was dead-beat for a smoke, he was more than generous with his cigarettes and when such times he could not afford to purchase any, then the numerous out-door cigarette machines in the area were compelled to meet his needs, simply by virtue that none of them could withstand the force of his huge fists.

Somehow childhood had given him the go-by. He was the only lad in the district, apart from my brother

Arthur, who was allowed to participate in the pitch-and-toss, and card schools, and consequently treated like an adult. He toted up his earnings from the wedding scrambles: "Three an'sevenpence av'made, Tommy," said he.

"Good heavens," I replied; that was nearly twice the amount that my father received from off the dole each week to feed and clothe me. We climbed up the bank and spent a few minutes watching the local pitmen playing quoits. Tiring of this occupation, we walked a few yards and stood in the doorway of the Blacksmith's shop.

The smithy, a strong looking individual aged about fifty, who possessed on his upper lip a moustache as wide and as thick as a new nail brush, was busy shoeing a huge cart horse, which I instantly recognised as belonging to the Corporation and was stabled in the lane next to my own. I had often assisted with another lad in cleaning out its stable; and the friendly creature earned its living by hauling around a large deep wooden cart in which was collected the household refuse of Benwell. Ginger confirmed my thoughts by pointing to the white circle on its forehead: "That's th'horse that cums round for th'dustbins, Tommy," said he.

The smithy looked up a second from his task. "Hellow, Ginger, had a gud day over th'road?" Ginger, was quite a local character, and everyone of an enlightened nature liked him.

"Two an'fourpence av'made," said he, without a moments hesitation. "Now," thought I, "that was the only way to tell a lie — like a real professional."

"How about a fag then?" inquired the smithy. Ginger entered the workshop, taking out his Woodbines from his trouser pocket, he placed one between the smithy's lips, put one behind his ear for later, and served himself one. Picking up a piece of paper from off the floor he went over to the furnace, pressed down on the bellows gently, lit the paper, then the smithy's fag and his own.

Slowly I edged myself into the workshop, until I too was near the scene of activity. The horse turned its head towards me, and appearing to have its curiosity more or less satisfied, returned its gaze on to the smithy, as though determined to keep a close observation on him.

The aroma inside the shop was the smell of hoof being singed with the hot iron shoes. The smithy glanced up again, this time at me: "Well, nipper, I see you don't smoke; and yer have a gud pair of shoulders on yer. Tell yer what, go over to the furnace there an'put yer foot on th'bellows, an'press up an'doon until I tell yer t'stop, pretend yer playin'the organ in th'church over th'road."

I moved over towards the forge and set to work. Blue and red flames instantly shot up from the previously dull glow of the coal-slack, as a result of my efforts on the bellows. Soon I had a good old fire gleaming, sparks, and thick smoke rushing up the chimney; creating to me the image of a miniature hell at work. I then observed another large horse shoe embedded in a halo of colours every bit as bright as a rainbow; the iron shoe then turned white with the heat I was stoking up. By now I had forsaken my earlier resolution of that morning, to become a singer; when I grew up I was now determined to become a blacksmith, and develop huge shoulders and strong arms; and devote my life to make a horse's one, a happy and well shod existence.

"Dosn't it hurt th'horse's, mister, knockin'them nails into their feet," I remarked.

He smiled at me, but made no comment, so I assumed I had asked one of my daft questions again. When he took the other shoe from out of the forge, I sat down on a wooden block. "My goodness," thought I, "If playing the organ was as tiring to one's legs as this bellows exercise was, then I assumed the man who played the organ in the Parish church on weekends must be sick of his occupation."

"How many are there in your family, nipper?" he inquired of me. "Ten," replied I, "six lads, two sisters, an'me mother an'da."

He shook his head in apparent dismay or perhaps disbelief.

"Ten eh, my God, they will tak'sum feedin. Luk, why don't yer git a paper job an'help yer mother to mak'ends meet?"

"Nebody wants any lads," replied I, never having ever given such a proposition any thought.

"Do yer know where Pendower Way is?" said he, laying down his hammer on the anvil, and picking up a large file with which he began to file away at the rough edges of the horse's hoof.

I replied in the affirmative, by a nod of my head.

"Well then, nipper, there's a paper shop on Benwell Lane facing Pendower Way, an'they're advertisin'in the'window for a delivery lad."

I stood up on the spur of the moment, eager at the thought of having a regular job and a wage to give my mother every week, which would help to make ends meet!

"Thanks, mister," said I gratefully. "I'll be seein'you, Ginger," and off I went over the quarry, through the allotments and out on to the terrace beside Pendower Way. Crossing to the other side to the newsagents, I noted with pleasure that the advert was still in the window. Inside, behind the counter was a woman serving a man with cigarettes. She appeared to be about the same age as my mother; dressed in a colourful shop coat. When the customer left I spoke up: "Can I have that job that's in th'window. Missus, please?"

She looked over and down on me, complete surprise registered on her face; then smiled, but still held her counsel, continuing to weigh me up. "Am strong, Missus, an'I can run faster than any tramcar in Benwell," said I, hoping to influence her decision by my eagerness.

"How old are you, son?" said she, finally. "How old have yer t'be?" replied I. "Thirteen," said she.

At the time I had recently been elevated to the senior classes at school, and had naturally thought the fact was sufficient to qualify me for the job; until she had answered my inquiry. "Am nearly thirteen," said I, firmly; adding eighteen months on to my age.

"You're small if you're nearly thirteen," said she, "Wait there, son, I'll go and bring my husband, he's the one who decides."

The door leading from the shop into the living quarters was wide open; all she had to do, in my opinion, was to give her man a shout; but up the four steps she went into the house; so I supposed she wished to utter a few words in his ear, and my hopes of getting the job sank.

She soon returned, her husband following. He was of medium height, with boyish brown hair, and a dreamy far-away look in his eyes. He was holding a briar pipe in one hand, and a pen in the other. The knot in his wool tie was as large as a tennis ball, and his spectacle frames too appeared to be out of all proportion. Somehow my confidence returned, I felt her husband was obviously eccentric; and I got on very well with eccentrics; I ran messages for quite a number of such characters in my neighbourhood.

"You're small aren't you?" said he removing his spectacles, and peering at me with a humorous twinkle in his eyes. "You say your nearly thirteen? Hm, well your'e going to make a fine steeplechase jockey some day."

"Am a gud worker, Sir, an'I'm the fastest kid in Benwell. Av told yer Missus I can beat any tramcar, that shows how quick I am."

"Tell you what, Tich, I'll put you on a week's trial, seeing that you're eager, though mind you it is against my judgement. Can you start in the morning at seven?"

A fat lot I cared for his judgement, I knew even without experience, I could deliver every newspaper that entered his shop, and still get to school in time to hear the morning prayer being recited in the main hall.

"I'm used t'gettin'up early, sir. I do al'the messages before I gan t'school." I thanked them both kindly and left the shop, hurrying along the terrace towards the co-op, to meet my mother.

As I was approaching my rendezvous. I observed someone in a deep-sea diving outfit, parading along the terrace, with a placard round his neck; advertising the appearance at the Grand cinema of the film, "20,000 Leagues Under The Sea". Of course some of the local lads, those who probably could not afford to go to the afternoon matinee, were tormenting the poor man, one or two throwing tin cans at him, knowing full well he was unable to retaliate, in the heavy gear he was wearing. What a way to earn a few coppers, he would have been far wiser to attend the wedding hoy-oots. The owner of the Grand, a Mr. Grantham, was certainly a colourful character; whenever it came round to local elections, he always got his agent to organise all the local kids to march round Benwell with his banners, and having us chant: "Vote vote vote for Mr. Grantham, Grantham is sure to win today; So we'll buy a penny gun, and make his opponents run, and Mr. Grantham will pay us all today." And of course he always kept winning with such organisation; so much so that he finally became Lord Mayor of the city and we kids were paid with a free treat for assisting him.

When I arrived at the co-op, my mother was waiting for me, with two large carrier bags, and a wooden box; my mother could always score for a wooden box at the co-op, yet I could not, I could never fathom this. "Ma, av'got a job deliverin'papers," said I, hoping to please her.

"Have you, hinny, that's good, but you're a bit young," replied she.

As usual, my father had to be consulted first on the subject. I handed her a shillings worth of coppers, and kept twopence for myself: "Don't tell me da, I've been to th'weddin'hoy-oots," I remarked.

To my surprise he agreed to let me take on the job: "How much is he going to pay you, son?"

"I don't know da, I never asked," replied I.

"You silly little nit," said he. "Listen, son, before you ever take on a job in the future, always enquire what the wages are; let the boss realise you have your wits about you, otherwise people will begin to think you're a half-wit, understand?"

"Yes, da I'll remember next time," replied I. My father was always liberal with his compliments; I don't suppose he really meant to sound too critical or hurtful, but I must assume he must have thought then that I was a little thick-skinned.

Next morning my father reminded me to enquire about the wage; Quietly I went down the front stairs, it being a Sunday morning, I saw no need to disturb any of our neighbours; selfishness was not part of my make-up. The newsagent was busy marking the papers when I entered the shop.

"Gud mornin', Sir," said I, full of first morning eagerness on a new job.

"Good morning, Tich," he replied, none too enthusiastically, I thought. He came from behind his side of the counter, and lifted a bag full of papers on to my sturdy shoulders, which reached down to my ankles. Every move I made my ankles received a sharp jab.

"Start from the inner side of the bag, Tich; Ridley Avenue — Jenison, then Dorcas, and so on, got the idea?"

I nodded, realising full well that my scant breakfast of dripping and bread was going to be put to the test; for the weight that was on my shoulders, I felt sure, would have even aggravated a donkey.

When I left the shop I sensed he was watching me out of the window as I crossed the tramlines; and the bag kept swinging in between my ankles, and it took all my effort to prevent myself from tripping over.

I was certainly looking forward to delivering the last newspaper on my round. A lady at one end of Jenison Avenue, opened her front door as soon as I entered her gateway; she presented me with, not a bacon sandwich which I was in need of, but a chunk of cherry cake; however I thanked her kindly, for I was in need of some form of sustenance. When I arrived back at the shop I thought the boss was going to have a fit. He rushed from behind the counter and anxiously peered into my bag. "What's the matter, Tich, why are you back so early?"

"Av finished, sir," replied I, wondering why he was so agitated. He called out to his wife, who quickly entered the shop, from the quarters, giving me a glance, as though I'd been discovered shop-lifting.

"He's finished the round, he says," said he, to his wife. "Impossible," she replied, "He's the first one back."

"Av delivered al'the papers," said I, attempting to reassure them, "I told you yesterday I'm fast."

"Are you sure you've never delivered papers before, Tich?" enquired he, a little hopefully I think.

"Niver once, Mister, this is th'first time, but its nee different than runnin'messages, an'I've done plenty of them. Me da says, I've got t' ask what my wages are?"

"Well, without counting your Saturday night specials, three and sixpence a week," said he, still appearing a little bewildered.

Off I went along the terrace towards home hoping there would be none of the regular Sunday morning senna-pods left when I got there; I was more than confident that my bowels required no artificial encouragement, after such morning exercise.

We possessed neither wireless or gramophone; but a number of times we were given a few nightly musical treats, when my father, on his week-day searches round the city for lumber, somehow managed to bring home some second-hand banjo, or concertina; and on one occasion an accordion.

He was a fair player of all those three musical instruments, including the mouth organ. It puzzled me in later years, with such talent, including that of a fine tenor voice, why he had not gone busking; it would have been more rewarding than pulling a handcart round all day, sometimes in vain, not earning one penny. Inevitably of course, every musical instrument he possessed at any given time had to be disposed of in order to purchase food.

Finally, a short while after I took up being a newsboy, my father returned home one night with a wireless, and then every Sunday morning afterwards we were entertained by such characters, as "Salty Sam the Sailor Man", and Big Bill Campbell and his Rocky Mountaineers, singing good old western songs in between passing the Applejack back and forwards to one another; by tuning in to Radio Luxembourg.

I think one has to experience living as one of a large family, denied of any form of games or other entertainment, and cramped of living space, for to appreciate what a difference that wireless made to our environment; friction almost ceased when it was turned on.

Another notable event took place about this period in my life, least it was notable for me. One day I had just entered the school dining room when the supervisor, approached me and asked me whether I would take over as dining hall monitor for that particular lunch time? I readily agreed, for to someone like myself who possessed such an enormous appetite, I was being given for one day at least, the opportunity to eat my fill. To my delight, next day, I was promoted to the post permanently.

CHAPTER
SIX

Lunch Time Monitor

Five minutes to noon I stood up at my desk in the classroom, and my teacher gave me the usual nod of dismissal, and I left the room. Once outside the classroom I descended those stone steps four at a time, such was my urge to get inside the dining room first as usual. I was excused study (that's what the education authorities termed it), five minutes before the other hungry children in the classroom on account of my being promoted to dining room monitor. Being so, I was one of the last to be served lunch, however to be within smelling range and sight of those large containers of beef stew, pea soup, or shepherds pie, not forgetting the rice or currant pudding, was to me, more satisfying than listening to lectures on subjects, which now on reflection, were in my humble opinion, both useless and nonsensical.

The dining room supervisor, a tall middle-aged woman of stern appearance, but kind, when you got know her, especially so if she takes to you and I was one of her favourites, nodded to me as I entered, as did the three ladies that acted at the servery. As usual I was the first monitor to arrive but just, a lad called Wilkins came running in, but stopped in his tracks when the supervisor cast her eagle-like glance on him; again not a word spoken by anyone, only nods of the head as a form of greeting. In seconds the other monitors filed in, too many of them at once — so no nods! We all stood at the head of our respective tables, the same table every day. From outside, from above and from all quarters, dismissal bells rang out, and soon afterwards the hungry flock once more returned to the fold, to receive free nourishment, on account that their fathers were members of the large unemployed army with a house full of kiddies.

Ten at each table; then another peal, this time from the small hand bell of the supervisor, who stood in the middle of the long room near the servery, and automatically everyone closed their eyes even the three lady servers, no exception when grace is to be recited. Then the firm business-like voice of the supervisor, who incidentally, I have often witnessed discreetly, keeps her eyes wide open for observation purposes, and no doubt God tolerates this weakness of hers, says grace: "For what we are about to receive, may the Lord make us truly thankful," and the chorus — "A-men!" And by God, 'tis a fact, that all of us children were truly thankful, for without this grub allowance and the third of a pint of free milk during the mid-morning break, probably two thirds of us present in the hall, would probably have suffered from rickets. At the head of each table was a large soup plate containing ten pieces of white bread, and it is up to the monitor to see that each one at the table receives a piece each. Then off we

84

monitors get to work to earn our extras. Two plates at a time if it is stew, three if it is shepherd's pie, until each one was served and tucking in royally.

All my life I have loved witnessing worthy people eat their fill, and being a monitor it was my duty, a pleasant one, to watch those ten children feeding themselves; spoonful after spoonful, at a speed that would have impressed any ship's stoker, who may happen to be on piece-work; meanwhile my own stomach protested at being left out of the race, in the only way possible by rumbling away like distant thunder.

After a normal breakfast of one, sometimes two slices of bread and marge, at seven thirty, a number of us could visualise how poor Oliver Twist felt, when he dared to ask for more.

Often as I stood watching them enjoying themselves, I cultivated the habit of studying each one at my table in turn, in order to pass the time away! Now the lad who sat at the far end of the table on the left as I stand facing it, the one who it seemed could never prevent his nose dribbling into his stew, and who makes no attempt in doing so not even by using his jersey sleeve, has the habit of folding his left arm completely around his plate, and keeps giving a nervous glance to left and to right of him as though afraid someone may snatch his plate away, is called Redhead. He is the champion grub polisher in the dining room, and can knock spots off my own record, which is admitting something. I always firmly believed that he would have been capable of devouring the contents of every plate on the table if he had of been given the opportunity. I could recall once, when both of us were awarded a week's free holiday at the "Lord Mayor's Holiday Camp" for poor children, at Amble. One day after lunch both of us volunteered to wash up in the kitchen, and very little of the leavings from lunch that day ended up in the camp swill bins. I had thought I could eat some, until I witnessed him that afternoon in that kitchen. It was a pleasure to watch him; and incidentally as is often the case with individuals who appear to possess abnormal appetites, he was as thin as a rake.

At eleven years of age Redhead appeared to suffer from religious fancies! On the way to school, he had to pass by two churches, and each of them had a "Thought For The Day" verse, posted up on its outside notice board. Redhead, whom I'm convinced, through some kind of inner fear, self created, always stopped to read each of the different verses, once, twice, three times, regardless whether the weather be rain, sleet, or snow. Then as he continued on his way to school, he muttered each verse separately to himself continuously, until he knew each by heart.

One morning he arrived in the classroom about ten minutes late, muttering to himself; and when the teacher inquired the reason of him being late, Redhead, began reciting one of these verses, and was actually beginning on to the second line of it, when he suddenly realised it. The teacher that morning was either in a leg-pulling mood, or perhaps just unconsciously demonstrating his ignorance, for he had poor Redhead in front of the class, quizzing him, and within a few minutes all of us learned, that for him to read these religious posters, morning and evening, was a compulsion. Indeed the habit appeared to have had such a grip on his personality, that wherever his parents sent him on an errand, he would actually go out of his way in order to pass by any church that advertised those verses. Failure to do so, he thought, was a sin, and perhaps God would punish him for it. However as regarding this fad of his the teacher made a joke of it, so unfortunately Redhead got no assistance from that quarter; only his leg pulled unmercifully afterwards from some of the other children in the class.

The lad facing Redhead, at the table, was the slowest eater I ever set eyes upon, and never once did he score for second helpings; though incidentally, he never appeared to suffer from ill health; whether this was due to his eating his food slowly, I knew not then; but since, I think the possibilities of it being so to be high. MacLean had the reputation of being the class dunce. One teacher in particular, in the junior school, used to adopt one of the fashions of the middle ages, in dealing with him, by planting upon his head a cone-shaped hat, with the letter D in capital letter glaring out towards the rest of the class; and was often made to stand in a corner of the room behind the blackboard. Whether this treatment inflicted upon him was intended to cure him of his supposed simplicity, I, at least, never knew. He was also supposed to suffer from the affliction of colour blindness, according to this same teacher, who once made an example of him by parading him in front of us, while the teacher picked up five sticks of chalk of various colours; MacLean seemingly failed the test.

But when he was in the so-called art class on a Friday I discovered he was one of the best drawers in the class; and no trouble whatsoever with his colours. In my opinion, he had been taking the mickey out of the other teacher, as retaliation for her making him so conspicuous in front of the other children.

The truth was as I found out later, he had no interest at all in general education, excepting art. He was able to read and write, but apart from this small achievement, the other subjects bored him; but to avoid displaying this fact which he knew would earn him nothing but the leather, or the cane, he played the fool, and with complete success!

The lad who sat at my end of the table on my left, is called Armstrong; and known throughout the school as a scrapper. He is the same age as myself, slightly taller, but the same fighting weight. Yet if the occasion arises, which it does often, he will take off his jacket, roll up his sleeves, and fight anyone, regardless of any superior size and weight of his opponents. From the above information, one would assume that Armstrong was a natural aggressive sort of lad; but I think they would be wrong. His philosophy towards aggression, patiently related to me, much later when he was a young man, was, that providing he never provoked or attacked anyone, then no one ought to provoke or attack him. There appeared indeed to be within him a real fear of violence; however if anyone threatened to commit it against his person, he always felt compelled to resist by the only means he knew how, toe-to-toe, and fight it out; and this feeling or determination of his applied to

88

adults also. Once or twice he even took on his own father, who was quite a handful by any standard; I never ventured to inquire who came off best.

If a scrap took place in the school yard, outside the school, or at home in the back lane, he would stand and watch, fascinated by, I think, fear. The only worthwhile aspect of his scrapping abilities to remark upon was, if he ever witnessed a bully thrashing a weakling, then immediately his features would become distorted with anger; then off would come his jacket, sleeves up, and pushing his way into the centre of the ring, he would haul the weakling aside and take over; and I lost count of the number of times he performed this charity on behalf of a helpless victim. Mind you he did not always come off best in all these encounters, but so was his determination and his reputation, of restarting the next day, where he had been forced to submit the day previous, that very few of the school, or local toughs, ever fell foul of him!

Of the other seven lads at my table, they were like myself, not worth mentioning; they were all good eaters; and the free lunch and milk ration, were about all that interested them in the elementary education system. The children at each table appeared to race one another in their attempt to clear their plates first, in the hope that there might be second helpings; and with the exception of MacLean the slow eater, my crew nearly always scored for any seconds that were available.

From the day I was promoted to dining hall monitor, and thus assured of my fill every lunch time, I never forgot once the appetites of the other children at my table; I knew what it was like to rely perhaps on the whims of a monitor who couldn't care less; so I was ever alert, as soon as an empty plate was pushed towards me, I was over to that servery in a flash, and kept doing so until all were once more enjoying themselves again! At the age of eleven, I realised that most of us through various circumstances, were being denied useful education; so naturally I was determined we would have all the free grub and any other handout that could be had.

I'm proud to admit there was always a race among the kids to get to my table at lunch time, for no one ever left it hungry if I could help it.

After the dining room had been cleared of the main flock, and each monitor had cleared his own table, then we would all sit together at one table, each being served with as much thick stew or shepherd's pie, as would feed three navvies. Yet believe it or not, some of us went back for more; and followed this with a large helping of pudding covered in custard.

Now that I was employed delivering newspapers I would get three or four slices of dried bread and place some shepherd's pie in between them, to serve me for tea, so I could proceed direct to the newsagents on coming out of school in the evening.

Even during the school holiday, excepting Christmas, this free feeding continued. Often for the sake of that free lunch I wished that the education authorities would make school attendance compulsory seven days a week. The stomachs of the young are indeed elastic!

CHAPTER
SEVEN

The Grandfather Clock

Tick-tock-tick tock sounded the old grandfather clock! It made a very agreeable and rhythmical sound, but only when you perchance kicked its base, or subjected it to a good shaking; and believe me, it was ever so important that it sounded healthy when the right moment came along, for on its musical behaviour, depended the feeding of ten hungry mortals! It was the only object from among a load of lumber that had raised the hopes of my father. The year was 1935; I was eleven at the time, small but strong for my age. My father, on the particular day I am about to relate, inquired of me as to whether I would like a day from school to assist him in collecting some lumber from a house on the other side of the city. It was an offer to play the wag; but help me God if I had ever done so on my own initiative.

However to stay away from school was no mean decision to make, for in those far off days, I was forever fighting a continuous battle attempting to contain an ever increasing appetite, and to remain from school meant forgoing my free lunch.

It appeared that whilst my father had been on his way home the night previous with his empty barrow, having failed to collect any rags or scrap, some kind gentleman had beckoned on him to stop, and informed him, that if he was to present himself on the morrow with his handcart and a little help (me), to a certain address, then he would be given the opportunity to earn a few shillings perhaps.

Try as my parents did they could not provide all of us with the bare essentials of life on the meagre handout described as dole.

Both of us walked down town that morning having no carfare; but it was only two miles. My father was reasonably tall, I was a titch, but never once did he have to wait for me; he remarked to me that morning that my legs were like my stomach — elastic!

On the walk to town I occupied my mind by counting the number of pubs, churches, and pawnshops, on the road, the task really kept me busy. Going down Westgate Hill, my father discovered a penny in one of his waistcoat pockets, so he sent me into a shop: "Here son, pop in there and ask for two Woodbines, and a couple of matches." The shop concerned, was situated directly next to an undertaker's parlour; whether being so close to this solemn concern, affected the shopkeeper's outlook on life, I could only guess, needless to say, his countenance was pretty grim. He served me with the cigarettes, then told me to inform my dad to buy matches. I felt sorry for the man somehow; but not so my father, he cursed that shopkeeper and his ancestors for full five minutes, going down that hill; beautiful poetical curses they were; but I will refrain from repeating any of them.

Opposite the football ground, in Gallowgate, my father hired a barrow; he was known and trusted to pay the fee on returning it. I climbed up on to it, and he pulled it through the posh parts of Newcastle, along Jesmond, over Armstrong Bridge, and into High Heaton, a distance of another three miles; just as well my father cobbled his own shoes. The ironical thing about this slump business was, it compelled men to remain idle against their will; but my father loved work, he was most happy when he was at it; so I reckoned industry as it was then, were missing out on a good thing when they refused him the right to work. Arriving at the house concerned, we found a large black saloon car parked outside the gateway, and the gentleman sitting inside it, climbed out and greeted us. He led us into the house and through to a big back room overlooking a huge well kept garden.

My father viewed the lumber, and a sign of disappointment crept over his face; all there was, lay in a small heap in one corner of the room, but standing in the opposite corner, quiet, and not unlike a sentry on duty, if one allowed his imagination to wander a little, was a large grandfather clock!

"The clock is out of order — hopeless — old age, so take that as well," remarked the owner.

It was the first time in my life that I had ever been so close to such a huge domestic time mechanism, and it really fascinated me. However, I was soon reminded by my father that there were other things to do than stand and gape at a timepiece, that had apparently given up the ghost. We set-to and loaded up the cart with the little scrap there was, covering it with the cast off clothing, then carefully we carried out old granddad; and the owner of the empty house bid us good day, climbed into his car, and drove away in an obviously philanthropic mood.

The less said about the mood of my old man the better; needless to say, that when the narrow door of the clock flew open as we were lowering it to the ground and struck him on the chin, he retaliated with such a kick to the base of the clock, that I was amazed to learn he had not succeeded in putting his foot clean through it. Then to our surprise and delight, the old timer came back to life, as though in response; and perhaps to prove he was not beyond complete resuscitation.

The tone of the clock was beautiful, so much so that my father calmed down instantly. For a few minutes, we sat on the cart shafts listening peacefully to the tick-tocks. I gazed up to one of the large branches of the old tree in the front garden, where a host of sparrows were perched and were singing to their hearts content, as though keeping in tune to the rhythm of the clock. It was a fair sized front garden, though not as large as the secluded one at the rear of the house; the house itself, consisted of eight rooms, a huge kitchen, large bathroom, and two indoor toilets; it was an ideal home in my opinion for a family of ten! Yet, so we were

94

informed by the owner of it, he was handing it over to his sister, a spinster.

Sadly, old grandpa decided to return to his slumbers; this time my father adopted gentler tactics he shook the old fellow awake, and once more we were entertained to another ten minutes of tick-tock music; afterwards we carefully secured it on the handcart on top of the old clothing. "I know a dealer, son, who will pay me a pound or more, for this clock, if we can have it ticking long enough for us to unload it and then get smartly out of sight."

My father gave me definite instructions on what I had to do when we arrived at the second-hand dealer's shop he intended going to: which in effect was to ensure, discreetly, that I promoted sufficient movement on the cart in order to keep the clock ticking away.

When we set off, we learned that the movement of the cart also set off the clock in motion.

Two or three hundred yards from our starting point a small red van pulled up ahead of us. A tall prosperous looking gent got out, and beckoned on my father to stop. One thing about him that impressed me, was his moustache, it was the largest I had ever witnessed; and somehow it appeared to make him look really jovial, and I formed the instant impression he was a man always looking on the bright side of life. As soon as he mentioned he was interested in the clock, I set-to and began my P.T. instructions: with both hands holding on to the back of the cart, I bent my knees then straightened up, knees bent — straight! He cast his attention on to me, and the smile on his face broadened. "He knows what I am up to," thought I. Nonetheless I kept at it; my father's orders were never to be taken lightly.

The old clock was ticking merrily away, thoroughly enjoying the golden opportunity of proving that there was still life in him yet, despite the contrary opinion of its late owner, who had ungraciously cast him aside after perhaps rendering so many years of faithful tick-tock service. I ceased my exercise at the request of the gentleman, and he ran his hands smoothly, gently, lovingly over the length of the clock as though he was fondly stroking some pet animal.

He wasted no words on making up his mind. "If you wish to dispose of this timepiece, I will offer you two pounds-ten," said he.

My father, also for the sake of word economy, accepted instantly. "It's a deal, sir," replied he, winking at me with pleasure.

The three of us transferred old grandpa, still ticking, from the cart to the van. My father thanked him on receiving the money, and once more we set off in the direction of the city, and towards the scrap merchants. Once out of sight of the van my father urged me to jump up on the cart, and off he set at a gallop down a back lane; his speed was such, that at the time, I felt that not even "Wells Fargo" at their best could have equalled it.

Then imagine our panic when a few minutes later, despite having taken a few diversions, we heard the hooting of a car horn behind us. Once more the shining red van pulled up, this time alongside us.

"My God, you can travel, sir," said the jovial man as he climbed out of his van, "If I could move like that on foot with a handcart, I would sell this van tomorrow."

In his hand was a tin box measuring about twelve inches by four.

"You left this box in the bottom of the clock, there's about five bob's-worth of pennies inside so you may as well have them."

He got back into his van, and before driving away he gazed at my father with that good natured smile upon his face his eyes shining with humour, "By the way," he remarked, "I am a clockmaker, I will soon have old grandfather in fine fettle." He then cast his eyes on me, winked, waved his hand and drove away.

My father wiped the perspiration from off his forehead with his coat sleeve: "Well, son, take that as a lesson, and never attempt to pull a fast one on anyone, no matter how hard-up you may be in life." The first café we came to we entered. My father smoked in silence as I ate my toast and drank my tea. I wondered what the kids were having for school lunch? Then I wondered why a man spent fifty shillings on a clock that was too tired to tick for more than ten minutes at a time? And why a single woman intended living in an eight room house; occupying space which would be far more suitable for ten mortals to live in?

Next morning as I was going out of the door to school I inquired of my father: "Da, what excuse shall I give to my teacher for being off yesterday?"

"Tell him, son," he replied smiling, "that your father's ticker was playing him up, he'll understand!"

CHAPTER EIGHT

My First Visit to the Seaside

Newcastle is only about ten miles from the Coast, with its miles of soft sandy beaches; yet up until the age of eleven I had never set eyes upon the seaside. One or two of my pals were taken down once or twice every summer during the long school holidays, but in most cases they were either an only child, or one of two, at the most. Ten of us would have filled one railway carriage, and emptied my mother's purse of every penny that my father received from the dole to keep us a week.

We had just broke up from school for the summer holidays. Somehow, a message must have been passed along the grapevine, for one afternoon, the tall hearty looking parson, from the Bond Street Memorial Chapel, called on us. I knew this good man well, for I sold him firewood now and then. He was one of those rare characters who devoted a lot of spare time in doing the useful kind of charity work. One of the organisations he apparently assisted was the "Poor Children's Holiday Association" which had its headquarters in Percy Street, in the city. My father was out at the time, so my mother talked to him.

This kind man informed her that the Association were organising a trip to South Shields on the coming Saturday, and three tickets were being allocated to us.

My father decided on the three of us who would be allowed to go; myself, my brother John, and my elder sister Kitty; who would be placed in charge of us.

On being selected, I first of all had to convince my boss the newsagent, that a day at the seaside, after morning delivery, would assist in recharging my speed batteries. Although I had not been long employed by him at the time, he immediately convinced me how much he thought of my worth as the fastest news-kid on the payroll, by releasing me and promising not to deduct anything from my wages.

The great day arrived, and being an experienced early riser, a compulsory one unfortunately, I was up and dressed and washed, in that order, even before my father had budged, and that was no mean achievement; for I had known him having had a night's session on Bass, not get to bed before midnight, yet still be up as fresh as a schoolboy, next morning. I informed my father that I would go for the old bread before I went on my paper round.

When I arrived at the bakery, my friend the big fellah, was on duty. Of course I was well known and liked by all the bakery hands that I had become acquainted with through the years, but the big man was a gaffer, and he always served me well; and, by God, bread then was really the staff of life. "Hellow, Nipper," said he, greeting me with his usual charm, "A little early, aren't yer, an'all spruced up as well."

I suppose I did look kind of smart that morning, not a safety pin in sight. "Am gannin'to th'seaside today, for the first time in me life, after I do my mornin'papers of course."

He smiled, appearing pleased on my behalf. "Why, you lucky bugger, has yer da found work then?" He patted me on the head. .

"No, the 'P. C. H. A.' gave me muther three tickets for th'trip to South Shields." "Well, how much old bread this mornin', Nipper?"

"Six penneth please, 'cause it's the weekend," replied I. He took my two carrier bags and the money, and went over to the large bin where the unsold bread of the previous day was stored; and returned with them bulging.

He slipped a penny into my hand. "Here, Nipper, have a gud day, an' divint try to swim al'the way to Denmark when you're down there."

My father was pleased as punch with the number of loaves, and some teacakes, I had brought back from the bakery; going there was a job always reserved for me, in fact I think I was of the opinion that all the tasks were reserved for me, and accepted that it was my penalty for having the reputation of being so swift and efficient.

I devoured my ration of two slices of bread and jam, and drank half a pint of weak tea. As I was going out of the door my father reminded me of another task: "Don't forget, son, as you come back from your paper round, call into Duncan's, or the Hadrian's, and ask for three penneth of bacon-pieces."

"Yes, da," I replied, and thought, "bugger you." I saw no reason why he could not himself go; after all, he always picked out the lean pieces for himself, and left the fat for us, claiming it was more "nourishing". At nine thirty, the three of us were on the terrace, within minutes our meagre number had swollen to the size of a small army; all of us urgently waiting for the organisers, and our growing presence was causing quite a stir of interest among the passing shoppers.

When the leaders did arrive, the tall husky parson was prominent in their midst. He walked in to the middle of the road, and assisted by the local Bobbie, held up the traffic. Over the road we swarmed, then placed into marching order.

Soon we were heading down Frank Street direct to Elswick Station; all of us now singing a popular local ditty to the tune of Tipperary:

> It's a lang way to'the'pan shop,
> It's a lang way to'the'pan shop,
> Where al'th'mothers'gan
> It's a lang way to'gan;
> Good bye coat an' waist coat,
> Fairwall t'watch an'chain;
> An' if I divint keep an eye on me troosers,
> They' all gan th'same.

Doors and windows opened automatically on the route to the station; and more children joined on the

101

noisy but happy procession, waving their tickets above their heads to signify they were eligible to accompany the struggling army on its way to South Shields; and a day away from the back lanes and dustbins.

The calls from all the well-wishers in the street, my own family included among them, kept all of us in a fair state of excitement.

Now it was the turn of the busy traffic on Scotswood Road, to grind to a temporary halt. Tramcars, motor cars, buses, and the horse and carts; only the poor horses would gain by the compulsory stop.

At either side of the station entrance, stood an organiser, each with an ink pad and a stamper: and they began stamping the words P. C. H. A. on to the back of one of our hands on our showing our ticket: this was intended mainly as a means of identification in case anyone of us got lost down at the seaside. As soon as my right hand was stamped. I gently pushed my way into the station entrance, but I got pushed back again to the left: and before I could explain, the man standing there stamped my left hand. I decided to ignore the matter, comforting myself with the thought that I was off to South Shields on a day trip, and not an unfortunate French convict on the way to penal servitude on "Devils Island".

This was the first time that my brother and sister, and myself, had been so close up to a train, and I urged them to grab one of my hands, and off we ran along the platform to the first carriage behind the huge belching steam engine. But once we were locked securely inside the carriage of the train which had no corridor to it, we were not long in regretting our choice; with the steam, smoke and soot, rising from out of the engine's chimney, we were compelled to keep the carriage windows closed and could not add our voices to the chorus that was increasing in volume as the train puffed and hooted its departure from the small station.

"There's th'killin'shop," called out my brother John, as we steamed past the slaughter house.

"That's where th'tripe an'black puddin's cum from," called out another excited lad standing next to my brother.

About half an hour later we steamed into South Shields. The station, similar to the one we had departed from, appeared not to have been painted since the day it was erected.

Those of us who were making our first trip to the coast were amazed at the sight of the sea and the beach. I was convinced there was sufficient water here to fill a million poss tubs.

"So this is where th'builders git their sand from," remarked one lad behind me.

What a place to live in, I thought then, far better than roaming back lanes; playing marbles; and watching unemployed men playing pitch-and-toss.

We were marched directly to a long wooden hut situated on the promenade; and inside, the layout was identical to that of the school dining hall. The volunteers, bless them, soon got to work feeding us; a meat square, sandwiches, and cakes; but where on earth had these kind ladies learned to brew tea? Only by saturating it with sugar could I manage to drink it. It was so strong, in my opinion, that even Dr. Samuel Johnson who was, I was to learn, a friend of the teapot, would have been astounded at the potency. After we all had cleared the tables of every edible morsel in sight, the chief organiser stood up on a small stage, and gave us words of advice on safety first. "Back here at two thirty for tea." he said. And so we were released to find our own way about, unless one wished to join in communal games. We were not too keen, so the three of us took to the water's edge and bathed our feet.

Later we sat down near to where a boatman was organising short sea trips. I observed a large merchant ship followed by two tugs were passing the North and South piers, heading for the open sea. My brother suggested the three boats were perhaps intending to race one another.

A tall buxom young well dressed woman approached us. In her arms, was a bonny plump baby, which was gurgling and smiling contentedly; but trailing alongside her, bawling his head off, was a lad aged about seven or eight. She stopped beside us, looking down upon my sister for a few seconds; then she glanced at me and my brother. Appearing satisfied with her scrutiny, she smiled at my sister, and spoke: "I beg your pardon, my dear, would you be so awfully sweet as to do me a favour?" The three of us remained silent, looking up at her inquiringly.

She was a posh talker; and judging by the dress of her and the children, their clothes were certainly not purchased at Paddy's market, or any other second-hand rendezvous.

"Would you mind if I arsked you all to take my dear boy on a boat trip, he's afraid to go on his own, and I can't take him myself having the baby. Of course I'll pay for you all?"

I at least, sighed with relief, for I had thought she was intending to ask us to baby-sit, time she went for a walk.

"Of course we will, Missis," replied my sister, standing up, and beckoning on me and my brother to follow suit. The lady handed a florin to her, and off we went towards the boatman, the stranger taking hold of my sister's hand, time his mother sat down on the sand with the baby.

The boatman was observing our approach with a knowing smile upon his face: "I see you've got a job, pet," he remarked to my sister, and glancing to our charge, who was busy drying his eyes on his shirt sleeve. When we got so far out on the water, he appeared afraid of being so far from land, and held on to the arm of my sister as though to reassure himself by doing so he would be secure. Then suddenly he relaxed, and joy beamed in his eyes; but what a pale face he had; yet he looked sturdy enough for his age. When he did decide to speak, he addressed my sister only, ignoring anyone else in the boat who made to talk to him. He observed the letters P. C. H. A. on the back of my sister's left hand: "What do those words stand for?" inquired he.

My sister appeared as though she was too shy to admit we were on a charity trip. "It means 'Poor Children's Holiday Association'," said I, "and it cost us nowt t'cum doon here, an'nowt t'gan back either." He glanced at me in a sulking manner, because I had spoken in place of my sister. Nevertheless he continued to address her and ignored me. "Why are you poor, then?" he inquired further, of her.

"Because me da can't find work," replied I, determined to remain the official spokesman on behalf of the family.

The boatman, leaning forward then backwards, as he pulled at the oars, was listening in to the cross-questioning taking place, an amused look in his eyes. He was a strong looking character. His face, neck and hands, appeared to be made of deep tanned leather, and his eyes I believe were a shade of green, they were kind and laughing eyes; a probable lifetime of hard work had not succeeded in damping down his interest or zest for life. I pictured him in my mind as resembling "Salty Sam the Sailor-Man" of Radio Luxembourg fame.

"What kind of work does yer da do, sonny?" inquired the boatman, of our charge.

"My da has a lot of houses," replied he proudly. The boatman carried on pulling at the oars, still smiling, appearing unconcerned and unmoved at the fact.

"If yer da cums up wore street, he'll git chased," remarked my brother to the lad, "'cause where we live — we chase al'landlords an'ticket men."

When we arrived back on the beach, he ran straight to his mother, and informed her that we intended chasing his da down the street on account of him being a landlord. His mother gave all of us a glum look, then took hold of her son's hand and walked away without saying a word. When they were about twelve yards away the laddie turned around and waved a fist in our direction. "No sense of humour," thought I. At two thirty we returned to the hut for our afternoon tea.

By three o'clock, we were let loose again, after having been warned we must return at four thirty for the journey home.

I was now in an explorative mood; we had already covered the beach from one end to the other; and now I was determined to explore the town to find out whether the inhabitants of South Shields were any different from those in Newcastle. Despite my sister's protests, off I went, leaving the two of them on the beach.

On the road leading into the town I was halted in my tracks by an old gentleman dressed all in black clothes, sailor fashion. His white beard practically concealed the whole of his face; only his smiling but mischievous looking eyes, and nose were visible. "Who learned you to walk so quick?" inquired he, peering down at me.

"I don't know," I replied, "But I can walk nearly as quick as me da."

"I used to walk as quick as you matey — ah indeed I did. Yes, for your size you walk quick. Are you in a hurry or somethin'?"

"Am gannin't'look around th'toon, an'see what it luks like, cause av'got t'be back on th'beach by half past four."

"For what there is in the town for you, matey, you may as well turn round an'go back to the beach now. If you like wanderin' you ought to go to sea. Get your father to sign you on a ship as a deck boy. I've been right round the world dozens of times — what do you think of that, matey?"

I think you're a bloody liar, thought I, convinced he was exaggerating on the number of trips he had made around the globe. "Did yer ever see any Pirates at sea, Mister?" I inquired. His countenance completely changed instantly, and he looked down on me as though I had suddenly decided to become impertinent towards him.

"Pirates!" he exclaimed with such force, that a number of passers-by, turned their heads in our direction to view the pair of us.

"Pirates belong to the history books, dosen't your teacher tell you that? I met rogues and vagabonds at sea matey, an fools." he more or less added and emphasised, as though referring particularly to myself, "but no Pirates. Well, matey, I can't stand here all day," and off he strolled without as much as a farewell.

The silly bugger, thought I, as though I wanted him to stand all day denying the fact, that there were still pirates on the high seas.

Outside a pub in the town I stood listening to an organ grinder. His small monkey with a chain around its waist, was sitting on top of the organ, busy eating a banana. "If you can afford fruit, the pair of you are doing all right," said I to myself. The organ grinder, a fat man, wearing a large trilby hat, was continuously turning the handle of his machine; and judging by his countenance, I took him to be an Italian, or a Gipsy.

Attracted by the monkey's gestures, he turned round towards me, and smiled, then beckoned on me.

"You look-a after my organ, please — yes — just time ha-go to toilet?" "Right, Mister," said I, eagerly. "Shall I keep turnin'th'handle?"

He lifted his hat to me — like a model gentleman. "That's da good boy, yes, you doos that," and off he went into the pub.

As I began turning the handle, the monkey attempted to search my head as though intending to look for fleas. "There's no nits in my head, Long-tail," said I, to it. Now whether my refusal to have my head examined, or whether my addressing him as Long-tail, had upset him, I could not say, but it immediately began jabbering away, and attempted to strike me with its small collecting bucket. But when a lady approached the organ and placed a penny into its tin, it calmed down instantly, and took out the coin, giving that a thorough examination instead.

When the organ grinder returned, I had increased his fortune by threepence. He patted me on the head, glanced into the collecting bucket, shrugged his shoulders, and thanked me kindly.

So off I went to resume my exploring. After what I took to be a thorough search of the town; I fell to wondering where on earth in South Shields did the posh people live? For the area I had covered reminded me of my own district! On each street corner stood the inevitable group of sad looking men, appearing as forlorn as their unfortunate brothers up in Newcastle. I could not help believing these unhappy men would be far better off to desert their posts, which they seemed to assemble to every day, as though by doing so they qualified themselves for their weekly benefit, and go on to the beach and gaze out to sea, and dream of far-away places of a make-believe land, where there was no compulsory idleness and its subsequent misery, and poverty.

Of the streets of working-class houses well, I could only assume that identical architects, and builders, the type who had planned and built the rabbit hutches, up in my district, were responsible for the erection of these eye-sores. Surely in a rational society, such men would or should be prosecuted for displaying total disrespect to their professions, and for displaying such callous contempt for these unfortunate enough to have to live in such unhealthy and unbeautiful buildings.

Apparently, so intent was I on my sociological research, that I lost my way, and by the time I decided to ask my way back to the beach, I discovered it was after five o'clock. I ran all the way back to the sea front; the hut was locked up; and I searched the beach in vain for anyone else having the letters P. C. H. A., stamped on the back of one of their hands. On my way to the railway station to inquire whether I could thumb a lift back on the first available train, I accosted a policeman, to ask his opinion on the matter. To my surprise, I learned that he was looking for me; and he appeared to be pleased at the distraction from pounding his beat.

At the Police station, the Sergeant invited me behind the counter and directed me to sit down.

For the first and perhaps the last time in my life, I received what was, in my boyish opinion, V.I.P. treatment. I was fed; and phone calls began to be made all around me, concerning my recovery, and my return to Newcastle. At long last, my contributions towards "helping to make ends meet", at home, was being recognised.

"Are you a good scholar, then?" inquired the Sergeant.

"Am gud at history, an'composition," I replied.

"But you're no good at keeping appointments, are you, hinny?" he retorted, "This is not four thirty, is it?"

I decided to ignore his remarks, and ask questions myself: "I hope yer send me home by train, Sir, cause if I git taken yem in a pleece car, th'people in wore street will think av dun somethin' wrang."

"Don't worry about the folks in the street for everybody will know by now you're missing from the trip," he replied.

My father was polite as could be to the Police escort, when we arrived; but he did not fool me. Once they had left, he began calling me every abusive name his tongue could lay hold of, and as a result, spoiled what up to then had been the most interesting day in my young life.

I undressed and climbed into the double bed, searching for a vacant space; muttering inwardly, that I would put his bait up when I grew up.

CHAPTER
NINE

Chasing the Blackshirts

Whoever invented the double bed, I feel confident, that he or she, did not intend that it would serve as a nightly resting place for five humans to kip in. Four of us older lads shared one of the double beds with my father; two down at one end, three at the other. Once my father came to bed, then that was practically the end of free movement for the four of us for the rest of the night. He could turn about whenever he felt like doing so, but not us, the command was "lie still" despite the fact that one of us may have someone's big toe partly up our nostril, or in our ear.

"Time to get up, Tom." I heard my father's advice although I was only half awake. "Yes, da." I sleepily replied, attempting to ignore him. "Time to get up," he repeated.

Again I made to ignore his command, not knowing what kind of mood he had awoken in. On account of my being the first of the lads to rise in the mornings due to being a paper-lad, my place in the bed was at the front of it. Without warning, my father's foot was against my back, I landed on the floor a few inches from the old heavy brass fender. "Up when I tell you," said he, apparently unconcerned whether I was still conscious or not. The cold lino was very bracing; I sprang to my feet and began searching on the old rocking chair, sorting out my trousers and jersey, from the pile of similar articles resting on it; I had my shirt on as I always slept in it. As soon as I had my trousers on I got down on my knees and crawled under the bed to seek my boots. My father slipped out of bed and into his trousers, then went out on to the stair head to fill the kettle, when he had it on the gas stove, he went back on to the stair head to wash. My old man was a cold water fanatic; he shared the belief of one of his literary heroes, Bernard Shaw, that it was excellent early morning treatment for the blood; and of course the colder the water was, the more he threw over himself; naturally he encouraged every one of us lads to follow the practice. Whilst he praised such treatment, we cursed it; not within his hearing, for curses were solely his prerogative.

He made the tea, and poured me out a mugful, and cut me a thick slice of bread, damping it with water and spreading a spoonful of sugar over it. "There's your breakfast, son."

"Ta, da." I swilled the tea down, the hotter the better, After I ate my bread, my father taking an old sack from out of the cupboard secured it around my shoulders with the aid of a large safety pin; it was raining heavy outside. As I was going out the door, my father spoke: "Don't forget, Tom, when you finish your papers, go straight to Jennings for the old bread." he handed me the carrier bag and threepence, then as an afterthought, gave me a halfpenny for the tram. I nodded to him. But unfortunately, that was another fatal mistake anyone of us in the family could make in his presence; for he always assumed that such lifeless gestures as a nod of the head were indications of sulking. My father was the type who required, and insisted on vocal sounds, in response to a question or inquiry of his: "Speak when I talk to you," he growled.

"Yes, da — I won't forget." I closed the room door behind me, and went down the stairs on to the front street; the rain was still falling heavy and the wind strong. I could not for the life of me understand why people required newspapers so early in the morning; we could not afford one and somehow got by without. My father visited the public library whenever he had the time and the need to consult the press.

When I reached the terrace, a tramcar was approaching in my direction, so I whipped over the road and jumped on it. Considering it was coming away from the town and heading towards its terminal point, it was practically empty, so I had to pay my fare, it would have been hopeless attempting to dodge the conductor under the circumstances.

When I arrived at my stop, I made to disembark by the door beside the driver which was quite in order normally, but on account of the bad weather he had it secured so as to suffer no discomfort. "What yer playin'at, Skipper?" I inquired, "Makin'th'customers use th'back door al'th'time?" He looked down on me, and with a growl rumbling from his nicotined throat, beckoned towards the rear door with a thumb. "That's your way off, yer parish-fed bugger, go on hurry up yer little waster." By now there were no other passengers on board, so no doubt he was giving vent to his dampened feelings on such a morning.

"If yer cal'me a waster agen, al'bring me da t'yer, an'he'll bash yer — 'cause he has nee Woodbines!"

I made my way back along the car and he shook his fist in my direction, he appeared to be in a hell-ava mood. "Bugger off an' deliver yer papers," he called out after me. The conductor remained neutral, and sat counting the takings, placing the coins into various paper bags. As I jumped off the tram I retorted shaking my fist, "Well, git away then, are yer ganin't'stay here al'day?"

I entered the shop, and my boss immediately came round to me, and placed the large bag of papers on to my shoulders. I glanced up at him, in a sort of meditative mood. He was only in his thirties and although it was a little stormy outside, it was still mild, yet inside the shop it was nearly as hot as the inside of Jennings the bakery. He was wearing two pullovers and sipping hot cocoa from a pint mug. Once he had remarked in my presence, that he loved nothing more dearly than sleeping under canvas. "That's what I term sleeping rough," he had concluded. "Sleeping rough," thought I, at the time, "I would have liked him to sample kipping in a double bed, with feet on his head and back, unable to turn over, he would then know what sleeping rough meant."

"There you are, Tich, you're always on time, I wish I had another half dozen like you. Don't forget keep the papers dry."

I left the shop and plodded my way up Sunnibank. Every morning on my round, at the same place, and the same time, this tall thin character, waited patiently for me, in order to tap me for a quick glance at the racing page. He possessed a fine soft voice low, yet I could hear every word he spoke so plainly, and his manners, coupled with his so-correct appearance, indicated the profession he had been employed in in the past, a butler. "Could I please glance at the racing card, my fine young man, only a few seconds; and remember I am to see you at Christmas, to render my appreciation." He was, so he claimed, at the beginning of our acquaintance, "temporarily embarrassed financially, but he knew better times were just around the corner". If his finances ever did improve during the time I knew him, he never let on about it to me, but purchase a newspaper, he never did to my knowledge. However at Christmas times he gave me an apple and orange.

Despite the weather, I was still back at the shop first, and at my usual time. I was kind of proud of my unbroken record, considering I was the smallest kid on the payroll, and carried, in my estimation, the largest bag, which incidentally had been purchased specially for me, as I was considered by the boss, as his Star boy. Though I must put it on record, he never backed up this confidence he claimed he had in me, by giving me a star wage. Sometimes I thought his failure to do so, was simply because he looked upon me as a joker, someone not to be taken seriously; and the way I grafted, for the wage I received, then he must have been right!

Handing over my empty bag, I left the shop, and ran over the road to the tram stop, where a tram full of fortunate workers was about to move off in the direction of the city. I jumped on the second step, crouched down low and hung on tight. I jumped off at Beech Street, and made my way up to the bakery. "Hellow, Nipper, finished your papers son? Old breed eh? Yes, I think I can manage that for a little workin' man like yerself."

After breakfast my father examined my footwear. "Well, son, as you're a monitor, you had better go to school, so wear John's shoes, he can stay at home and play with his baby sister, and I'll have your shoes dry for tonight so as you can do your paper round."

This decision made my brother protest, for as far as foul weather was concerned, he had the aptitude of a Yukon prospector. He would tolerate willingly snow blizzards, and rain storms, twelve months of the year, and remaining indoors would be like subjecting him to a good whipping; and I reckoned, if he didn't cease protesting, whipping is what he would receive; my father would not tolerate dissenters, in his family. None of us were ever allowed to go to school without some form of covering to our feet; I once went in my bare feet, and got sent home. Of course many a time I went the errands with nothing on my feet in order to save whatever footwear I did possess at the time. It stands to reason, no child could be fed and clothed on two shillings a week. The members of the appropriate government committees who sat and deliberated on such matters, and subsequently agreed on such an unrealistic sum to be paid for the upkeep of a growing child, were as naive as the ancient scribes who attributed the feeding of the multitude by Jesus with five loaves and two fishes.

There were three of us delivering newspapers in the same area, each of us employed by a separate newsagent, which could at times prove a little difficult. Lanky for instance, he had a healthy thirst for milk, other people's. He would lift a bottle of milk from the doorstep of one of his own customers, slip it into his bag, then conceal himself in some back garden and drink it, then throw the bottle into the garden or garbage bin. Sometimes he was having two pints a morning. Of course we other two lads were coming under suspicion. I had an idea that Lanky was the milk fiend; so on disclosing my opinion to this effect to the other lad, we decided to do a little bit of detective work, and to make it more interesting, we agreed that I would act the part of Sherlock Holmes, and the other lad to act the part of Dr. Watson.

Eventually one morning we caught Lanky in a back garden drinking a bottle of milk. As I had previously told this partner of mine in our recently formed detective business, that my paternal grandfather, had been a prize-fighter, he suggested cunningly, that I ought to be the one to give Lanky the tanning he deserved. Flattered no doubt by the confidence that my ally held in me, I hung my bag of papers onto a garden gate, rolled up my sleeves and let go with my right! I had up to that moment believed myself to be the fastest news-kid in the area; I was completely wrong, Lanky was terrific. Despite what feelings I may have stoked up within myself against him, and so suddenly, that when I witnessed him depart from my approaching right fist, as though carried away in a whirlwind, my heart swelled with pride, on realising that I had been fortunate, however short of an acquaintance, to have known a lad, who in my opinion, ran swifter than a greyhound.

After a while, I began giving a lot of thought to my newspaper job, and the number of hours I had to spend on it every week; and wondered if there was another, and easier way, to earn a wage, to assist in this business of making ends meet.

One Saturday morning on completing my round, I took my wages home as usual and received my threepence pocket money; then without disclosing my intentions to anyone, I took the sack out of the cupboard, the one which I used to wrap around my shoulders when it rained or snowed, placed the axe inside it, and left the house. Since I commenced delivering papers, I had found little time for my firewood business, and I realised I would have to start from scratch again in order to build up a regular round. With two boxes, I made my way to the quarry behind the Grand Cinema, and chopped them up into firewood.

I decided to make my first call at the Bond Street vicarage. The parson, answered the door himself and my luck was in obviously, for he appeared to be pleased to see me. The sack was large and quite full.

"Av started with me firewood agen, sir, if yer want any."

"Splendid! Splendid! How much have you in the sack?" he inquired.

"A shillin's worth, sir," said I. He hesitated a while and peered up towards the heavens as though he was seeking guidance on the matter.

"Alright — bring them in along to the scullery." He paid me, and told the maid to give me a rock bun.

Well, I was back in business. I returned on to the terrace in search of more boxes. So eager was I to prove to myself that I could earn in a day, as much as I earned in a week, climbing hills, with a large bag of newspapers trailing round my ankles, that I did not go home for lunch, but bought some chips, and then continued with building up my round; and even forgot about my intended visit to the Majestic, to see Tom Mix.

By two thirty, I had earned over three shillings, so I went home, placed the money on the table and asked my father whether I could pack up my paper deliveries. He shrugged his shoulders, then told me to sit down on the rocking chair. Providing me with a huge portion of stotty cake smothered with jam, he patiently sat down next to me, and gave me a ten minute lecture, a talk in which the names of Harry Pollit, and Karl Marx, cropped up; and I was urged to realise that we were living in hard times. As though I didn't know.

So I agreed to stick it out with the papers.

At the top of Atkinson Road, alongside the cemetery wall of the Parish church, in Benwell, was a favourite meeting place of most of the political parties in the area. On a platform, or a makeshift such as an empty crate; the Independent Labour Party; the Labour Party; the Communist Party, the Blackshirts; and one or two individuals, who felt they had a political message to deliver, held their meetings regularly. Why the Tories never turned up was anyone's guess.

I remember one summer evening; I was ten years old at the time, I wandered out of the back lane on my own and walked along the terrace, intending to go to the quarry, to look for some of my pals whom I believed were there, playing at cowboys. When I got as far as Atkinson Road, I observed a crowd of people standing around a platform, on which stood a middle-aged working man giving a socialist lecture. In a robust voice, he was busy laying into the government; and to judge from the response of his audience, they were in complete harmony with his bitter and scurrilous condemnation of it. I crossed the road and wormed my way into the inner circle. Although he possessed a strong voice, his physique somehow belied the fact; he was not very tall, and he appeared to have been born with a shortened leg, which was levelled by an oval plate of iron extending from the sole of his boot. Whatever his physical defects, I could appreciate he had a good headpiece on his shoulders. I soon gathered he was a socialist who could not somehow control his invective towards those comrades, who had worked their way up from the street corner, to the corridors of

121

power. Toe-rags, and lickspittlers, were two terms of abuse he favoured, when referring to these individual socialist celebrities, whom he claimed, had sold what ever working class principles they had formally held in exchange for banking accounts, and Whitehall honours. He even claimed, that Mosley, had been too left-wing, for the taste of some of these so-called socialist stalwarts.

What held me to the spot until the meeting closed, instead of continuing my journey to the quarry, I could not have answered then, except to say perhaps, that I found his performance exciting and entertaining. Though I did wonder at the time, what it would feel like standing up there on a platform lecturing in public? From where I stood I considered it to be a very lonely place!

How lonely, I found a few years later whilst on the "Road", and I climbed up on to a platform in Hyde Park Speakers' Corner, to indulge in a bit of spouting, time a brother tramp, whipped round the crowd making a quick collection in aid of our grub stakes, during the absence of the Police; for public collecting is not allowed in the park.

I think I admired his courage standing up there, facing a large crowd of mostly dissatisfied and unemployed men, who especially in the absence of any representative of the law, could possibly become quarrelsome and out of control.

Thereafter, I began to observe that the Police, often remained absent whenever an individual was exercising his right to say a few words on whatever topic suited their fancy. Though when an organised meeting took place on behalf of a political party, there was always one or two Policemen present; and their strength became noticeably increased whenever the National Socialists were expected to turn up; for it was the Blackshirts, with their para-military appearance, who always earned the most heated animosity of the spectators.

Although my father would never join any political party, he was a staunch believer in socialism; though towards the Labour party hierarchy, he always expressed nothing but contempt. Whenever he decided to stroll along the terrace and listen to any of the political meetings, I had to make myself inconspicuous, for he was of the opinion, and perhaps rightly so, that political meetings are no fit rendezvous for children; so on such occasions, when I was forewarned that he was going to be present, I would conceal myself up in some tree in the cemetery that overlooked the "speaker's corner". And if there happened to be a little scuffle, then that only went towards increasing the nights entertainment for us up in the tree-tops.

I came home from school one day and found my father had company. He was a tall well built man, who appeared to be about the same age of my father; also he was a bachelor; which I supposed then, was one of the reasons why he looked so well fed and content. My mother gave me my ration of bread and jam, and a mug of tea as soon as I entered; I always got served first because I had to go straight out afterwards to the newsagents.

As I chewed my bread, I listened in to the discussion being held between my father and his visitor. I gathered they were talking about the apparent increasing strength of the Blackshirts, in the country, and the stranger was voicing his opinion, that this fact was mainly due not only because of mass unemployment, but because their interests and progress, were being nourished by certain sections of the ruling class; including some politicians in high places. I also learned that there was to be a meeting of the Blackshirts, that night, along the terrace.

My mother, who had only recently returned from the public wash-house, after having done a hard afternoon's work at the posstub, where she had scrubbed, laundered, and dried, a whole week's washing, was going about her endless and thankless tasks, as though she was not paying any attention to the political discussion going on, but I felt sure she was, for she appeared anxious and uneasy at the presence of this husky firebrand, and I knew she would be pleased to see the back of him; yet she held her own counsel, and was wise not to voice any displeasure.

As I left the house, the stranger was remarking that he might join the International Brigade; for what purpose, or where he intended going, I never learned, for I had to run off to the paper shop.

When I returned home, and managed to get some more bread and jam I went outside in search of two of my pals, and related to them where I was heading for.

A crowd was gathering outside the cemetery wall, as the three of us went down the bank a little way,

124

and assisted each other over the wall and into the cemetery.

I immediately climbed up into my favourite tree, but the other two began pulling up grass clods, with the intention of throwing them over the wall on to the Blackshirts, if any trouble broke out.

Soon the meeting commenced, and after being introduced by the chairman, the main speaker took to the platform; immediately, the other uniformed Blackshirts ranged themselves around the platform as a token of security; their arms folded, and grim faced, each of them had that particular expression upon their countenance, that certain look which obviously was intended to warn any would-be adversary, "any nonsense and we know how to deal with it!"

And so the speaker commenced: "Comrades, I intend speaking tonight on the evils of unemployment." Which I thought was rather a related subject, considering practically everyone in sight, with the exception of the Police; two miners, whom I recognised were employed; and myself; were out of work.

He continued, informing his audience, how Germany was solving its unemployment problem. And then, for what appeared to me at that moment, an unrelated deviation; he began letting loose an obviously worked up venom towards Jews, and Communists; and he appeared to froth at the mouth whenever he mentioned either group of these alleged enemies of his.

Soon I gathered that in essence, the whole of his remarks on the evils of unemployment, and the cause of it, amounted to the blame being directly attributed to the curtailment of capital investment by the Jews.

The Communists came in for their share of his hatred, for which, in his view, they were creating unrest among the unemployed.

I was suddenly distracted from the speaker's remarks, on observing my two pals, down below in the cemetery, were apparently attempting to dislodge one of the old, gravestones. Jumping down from off my perch, I remonstrated with them: "Hav'yer nee respect at al'," said I. My chastising was cut short by the sudden sound of a rowdy commotion coming over the wall from the direction of the meeting. We all sprang up on the wall in time to witness that the meeting was being broken up in a frantic free-for-all. The speaker had been pulled down off his platform, and his bodyguard were in complete disarray. Despite the presence of the Police who were struggling to separate the two groups of antagonists, the superior number of anti-fascists coupled with their obvious united fury and determination, proved too much for those who were doing their utmost to resist, and the Police were forced temporarily to retreat, and the Blackshirts were chased out of sight!

I don't know whether the chasing of the Blackshirts, had been worth it; for about a week later, they marched along the terrace in full regalia, with a strong Police escort serving as bodyguard.

CHAPTER
TEN

The Musical Professor

A week before the school broke up for the Christmas holiday in 1935, my elder sister unfortunately contracted a complaint known as "ringworm". As though this was not bad enough, my father was having no luck at tatting, no one wished to be rid of any scrap or rags, before yuletide. The school board Officer, warned my father that none of us had to go out, even to go messages. The man was obviously devoid of imagination; as though my father would go for old bread, or bacon pieces, not to mention shoving newspapers through letter boxes.

All those weeks previous, we had faithfully attended Sunday school; and now we would be compelled to forego our free Christmas treat given by the respective churches.

On Christmas Eve, we secured a stocking apiece to the line across the mantle shelf by means of a safety pin, as usual; more out of habit than hope. We all knew by past experiences, and present circumstances, that the most we could expect to find in them would be an apple, orange and a few nuts! I was not lacking in imagination or romance, as regarding whether to believe in the existence of Santa Claus or not; but I was somehow overwhelmed with the fact that not once in my young lifetime, had he ever paid us a visit leaving anything faintly resembling a toy, a game, or a doll, for my sisters. He was no doubt a jolly old fellow; but he only paid Christmas visits to children, whose parents were more or less economically solvent.

On Christmas morning, we played on the floor with marbles; but the useless things were for ever rolling under the bed. With space being at a premium, more so on all of us being confined to the house, I would have sat under the bed if it had of been high enough from the floor to allow me to do so, if only for the sake of solitude, which I craved for, and to day-dream.

I was flat on my tummy under the bed searching for one of the marbles, when a knock sounded on the outer door. "Come in," called out my father. And in walked a scout master, and two boy scouts, each carrying a cardboard carton, which they placed on the table, and wished us a merry Xmas.

After they left, we discovered the cartons contained groceries, fruit and a game of draughts; the first game I had witnessed in the house. "God has strange ways of working," remarked my mother; as my father had expressed surprise as to how the local scouts had known of our existence, let alone our plight.

It proved at least to me, that some good Samaritan resided in the neighbourhood, and who went out of their way to speak on our behalf; for I had not forgot my summer trip to South Shields.

I stood at the window and gazed out at the large snowflakes falling thick and fast outside. I was busy imagining to myself, that the roofs on the other side of the lane were the outlines of my beleaguered fort, and the chimney pots, well, they were rows of white cannon, and I was a General in the Foreign Legion. Outside, it was sand, not snow, that was blowing about in a furious whirl; and my men and I, were cut-off, without food and only a little water; all of us hoping and praying that the relief column would reach us. But alas it was hopeless; behind me, my brothers and sisters were playing leap-frog, in the small space that separated the bed from the wall; and now the downstairs neighbours were knocking-up, as a gesture to less jumping.

Being the oldest lad in the room, as soon as I heard the door knob turn, I immediately turned my attention on to the flock, and I was in the throes of giving them all a dressing down, when my father entered. As I appeared to be chastising them, he refrained from calling me names. After warning us, he returned to the living room, and I followed him.

"Da, I have a sack full of sticks in the wash house, there's a shilling's worth, if yer let me gan oot, I'll sell them quick in this weather."

It was Saturday, and my mother was out shopping on the terrace. My father had previously decided that I had better remain indoors to keep my shoes dry, for my evening paper round. He turned from the fireplace, moving over to the window, which also looked out on the back way, and gazed out; after a while he spoke: "Tell you what to do, get ready, son, and put John's shoes on, and I'll loan you my old jacket, that should be as good as an overcoat for you."

Giving him no time to change his mind, I crept under the bed and searched for my brother's shoes, I was older than him but we practically took the same size; indeed, we had to!

As soon as I was ready, my father secured the large lapels of his jacket around my neck with a large safety pin; and despite my mild objection, he planted an old cap of his on to my head. I glanced into the mirror of the large old fashioned press, "What a bloody mess I look," thought I. The only consolation I felt, was that all my pals would be indoors, and would not witness my odd rig-out, for they were a tireless lot of critics. But I gave no sign of dissatisfaction, such was my eagerness to escape from the overcrowded billet; rather my spirits rose as did my imagination! No longer did I imagine myself to be a Foreign Legion Commander; I was now a North West Mountie, setting out on an explorative mission; having no horse, or skis; just a sack full of firewood; but thought I, what better essentials could a Mountie wish for than firewood, in weather such as it was.

Unseen by my father. I slipped the axe under the long jacket, and down the backstairs I went, collecting my firewood and placing the axe on top. Up the lane I went, excited as hell because my footfalls were the first to disturb the shroud of virgin snow. If only I could have heard the sound of one lone dog, howling out like a wolf, it would have about completed the silent white scene, and perhaps have drawn me spiritually at that moment to a particular story-teller, whom my father had recently acquainted us with, called Jack London.

I plodded my way along Gill Street and down into Bond Street to the vicarage. He purchased half of my firewood, and I sold the rest in the same street. After a search on the terrace, I scored for two boxes and took them into a back lane, where I chopped them up, despite the furious objections of some mongrel dog to my presence.

Once more I plodded on my way up Bond Street, past the wash house, and onto one of the roads leading to the West Road. Most of the inhabitants up there, so I heard, owned their own house, so it naturally impressed me that they must be better off than the inhabitants of my own locality.

The first prosperous looking house I called at, a gentleman came to the door, newspaper in hand, spectacles resting on the bridge of his nose, and wearing a dressing gown over his outdoor clothes, and slippers on his feet. He did not give me the opportunity to open my mouth; in one swift experienced glance he took in my whole shabby appearance: "I want no hawkers here, go away or I'll phone the Police," he slammed the door in my face, and quickly retreated to his front room window to observe my departure. I was rather surprised at his outburst; usually the non-buyers, just shake their heads, mutter "close the gate" if there was one, and vanish back indoors. However, I was determined not to be put-out by such ill humour. Nevertheless I was halfway up on the same side of the road without my having sold one penneth of wood,

131

when I decided that I must surely be on the wrong side of the road. So I crossed over, and entered the gateway directly in front of me, and pressed the doorbell. After a few seconds I heard the sound of music coming from inside, then soft footsteps approaching along the passageway. The door opened, and I was confronted with a man whom I had often observed on the terrace, and always appearing in a flurry; a violin case under his arm, and carrying a briefcase. He was an eccentric looking gent, of medium height, long silvery locks, and the most noticeable garment of his very tasteful dress, was his dazzling coloured waistcoat; he was the model of neat, but extravagant dress. And of course, I was his complete opposite, a model of a shabbily over-dressed juvenile old man; it was a classical case of one eccentric confronting another.

There was one thing that clearly attracted me, on being close to him for the first time, apart from his colourful raiment he possessed the most gentle and kindest eyes I had ever seen in a man.

"Ah — good afternoon, Sir," said he, smiling kindly. That was the first time I had ever been addressed as Sir, and it had the effect on me of a tonic.

"Do yer want any sticks, Mister, for the fire?"

He began rubbing his hands as though in sheer pleasure. "How extraordinary clever of you. How did you know I required firewood? Was it because it is snowing, and you perhaps assumed I could not get out to purchase any?"

I peered up into his eyes, thinking he may be taking the rise out of me; but he appeared sincere enough. At that moment the music inside the house began to fade out, then halt, and a scratching noise commenced. "Ah, excuse me, my good man, step into the doorway, I must attend to my gramophone, I shan't keep you waiting long."

He appeared to glide along the passage, and quickly returned. "Now then, Mister dealer, tell me, how much do you want for your firewood?"

"Ninepence, Sir, there's enough t'last yer a week," I replied eagerly, hoping he would purchase the lot, and save my feet from further cold punishment.

"Can you play draughts?" he suddenly inquired to my surprise.

"Yes, I can play, Mister," replied I, wondering what the playing of draughts had to do with the selling and purchasing of firewood.

"Tell you what I'll do, you come along inside and play me a game of draughts, and whether you win or lose, I promise I shall purchase all your firewood off you."

I followed him along the passage which he was determined to describe as the hallway, into his living room, which overlooked the backyard. A huge fire was burning in the grate, and to judge by the size of it, I reckoned he must have been burning a bucketful of coal at a time; such comforting extravagance delighted me.

Near the window stood a large gramophone, directly facing it against the wall was a well stocked bookshelf. Near the fireside were two leather covered straight-back chairs, on one of which lay a violin and a bow, on top of some sheet music; and apart from a small table and a leather covered armchair, there was no other furniture in the room; mind you there was an expensive looking carpet on the floor. A door on the left of the window led into the scullery, and he pointed to this door: "Place your sack through there, my good man." When I returned he invited me to take off my jacket and cap, and to sit on the vacant chair, time he brought the table over towards the fireplace, then left the room to seek the game.

He set the board out, allowing me the black pieces and the first move. There was no doubt in my mind he allowed me to win the first game, for he won the second game decisively. "Do you like music?" he inquired after the second game was over.

"Yes, Mister," I replied, as he set about placing a record upon the gramophone turntable.

"Now then, sir, I want you to make-believe you are at a musical concert," said he smiling, but no doubt being serious. "And the first thing to remember when at a concert is, that silence is golden. Talk if you wish, but only at the intervals, that understood?"

"Yes, sir," said I, rather curious; the only thing then that I could associate the term concert with was the stage shows that were periodically staged at the Grand cinema on Condercum Road, in place of films.

No sooner had the record commenced playing, than he instantly took up the violin, sat down, and within seconds he had in effect become part of the symphony orchestra of the record, which was rendering such

134

beautiful music, the likes of which I had not up to then heard before.

I had once heard my father, a few nights in succession, knock out a few melodious tunes on a fiddle, before the instrument had went the way of all cash convertible objects that entered our house; and I had been overwhelmed with awe. But the playing of this nattily dressed character, held me spellbound with pleasure. Time he played I felt certain that as far as he was concerned, I did not exist; he was on a plane of his own and I did not wonder why he had insisted on my silence from the beginning; though without his kind warning, I would not have dreamt of interrupting such heavenly music, for I was enjoying it every bit as much as the maestro himself.

When the music of the gramophone came to an end, and he had lain down his violin, and turned over the record, he turned to face me: "Well, young man, did you enjoy the music?"

"It was great, sir," said I, and I meant every word of it, more so he sensed this, for he appeared very pleased.

"Well, don't you wish to show your appreciation? Don't you wish to applaud by clapping your hands together?"

I felt myself uncontrollably carried along with his almost boyish enthusiasm, and began clapping my hands; after all he was entertaining me as well as himself. I had never realised up till then, that grown-ups could take off on such flights of fancy; if such behaviour was directly responsible for others to credit him as an eccentric, then I was all for eccentricity, at whatever age.

After winding up the gramophone and setting it to play once more, he resumed his seat and began playing his violin. At intervals during this piece of music he ceased playing the violin, and using his bow as a baton, took to conducting, and he appeared by every gesture of his make-shift baton and his free hand, as though he was conveying his own feelings towards the music, and to each individual section of his imaginary visible orchestra. I knew nothing about his music or what training he may have had, yet somehow I gathered his art of conducting was the real McCoy. His hands appeared to float, to fly and to gallop, with every note of the music; and his face was covered in a film of perspiration. His antics were fascinating, and as I watched him I was doing my utmost to weigh him up! There were times when I had thought my Uncle Charley was a card; but this man was terrific and I considered seriously, asking him to teach me to play the violin, so as I would have a profession to turn to when I grew up; for what education I was receiving, I would be only qualified to continue delivering newspapers and selling firewood.

Whilst he was selecting the second record to play, he revealed to me, he was a vegetarian; never smoked; but he had a liking for madeira wine! I was at a loss as to what the confessions should have conveyed to me. But if they meant in essence, that a vegetarian diet; being a non-smoker; and partaking in an occasional bottle of madeira, were the source of his undoubtedly boundless

136

energy, then alas I would still have remained at a loss. For I too was a human power-house, I could climb as efficiently and as swiftly as any monkey; outrun any tramcar, or Policeman; and work countless hours without feeling the least bit tired; and my main source of food, apart from the free lunch at school, consisted mostly of starchy food, tea, and a small amount of bruised fruit on a Saturday. Nevertheless, his remarks I stored safely away in my memory closet; for young as I was I realised that some people, especially butchers whose task it is to sell meat, gave too much credit to it as a food. Lack of means denied our family, and many others from becoming large meat eaters; but the professor here appeared to be very comfortably off, his waistcoat, and I am not being personal, must have cost at least three or four pounds; yet he refrained from eating meat, and he was a picture of glowing health, and simply oozing with energy.

"Well, that's the end of the concert, my good sir," said he, laying down his violin and bow on to the armchair. "Ah — my dear fellow, do you know what it is like — do you? I live for my music, I dream about it. Music is another form of poetry, only more intoxicating. Now then, I shall make some tea, then you must go home."

"Yes, I better go home," thought I. Otherwise my father would begin performing another form of music, using my head as one of the instruments; for, like "Pip of Great Expectations fame", I too was being brought up by hand — two hands as large as pan shovels!

From the scullery he brought in afternoon tea on a large silver tray; and the crockery was the most delicate and prettiest I had seen up to that moment. The more I praised the cake, the more he served me with; this learned musician, certainly knew how to cater to my normally starved tastes.

At the front door he shook hands with me, and invited me to return someday soon to listen to another of his concerts.

He closed his front door, I closed his gate; and then felt as though I had just left paradise in order to return to hell. The snow was still falling heavy; and somehow my brief introduction, however temporary, to spiritual, as well as material luxury, left me a little unsettled, and I was not looking forward in such weather to shoving newspapers through letter boxes.

One afternoon in 1936, as I was about to leave the classroom after the day's lessons, the teacher beckoned on me to remain behind. He then inquired whether I would like to go to the "Lord Mayor's Holiday Camp" at Amble, for a week. I was thrilled with the offer and gratefully accepted, so he gave me a letter to take home to my parents.

When I got home, I discovered my brother Arthur, had also been offered the same golden opportunity. Of course it was quite a struggle for our parents to don both of us out to look tidy; however prior to the great event, my father, from his tatting round, managed to dress us, and provide a decent pair of shoes each.

On the morning we departed, my mother gave each of us two shillings; the total sum that my father received from the dole to keep us, and we were most grateful, for she could not have possibly done more.

Whilst at the camp, and being ever on the look-out to earn a few coppers, I scored for the post of batman, to my teacher, who was quartered in a cubicle at the end of the wooden built dormitory.

I soon learned, as I daily made his bed, polished his shoes, and swept out his cubicle, that he had a fair liking for "wallop", and I saw to it that I got the job of taking the empties back.

One evening my father took me over the town moor, to listen to a political meeting which was being held to explain, and to gain support on behalf of Spanish refugee children. It was the largest public meeting I had ever attended, there appeared to be countless hundreds of people surrounding the high platform, and one of the main speakers I believe, was an active member of the International Brigade. A group of Spanish children sat on the grass in front of the platform; and they appeared in my eyes, sad looking kids, rather bewildered from being made the focus of so much attention from the sympathetic crowd.

As I walked back home, I thought, despite hard times, I am more fortunate than those poor buggers; separated from their parents, and their homeland; and a strong possibility they may never see their parents again, assuming they still lived. And of course if only two-bob a week was allowed for their welfare, as was our lot, then they were really in for a trying time, the poor devils.

Ever since the musical treat that I had experienced in the house of the Professor; the name I had mentally bestowed upon him; on that Saturday afternoon in the midst of a snow storm, I had often yearned for the opportunity to repeat the pleasure. It is true he had on my parting then, invited me to call again; and numerous times I did call on a Saturday afternoon with firewood as an excuse, but could never find him at home. A few weeks after that event, I had seen him on the terrace; but he had passed me by without giving me as much as a glance, and I had unwittingly taken the incident as a hint "to be seen but not to be heard".

Though I ought to have guessed that such was his preoccupation with his thoughts, that he could have passed by his own mother, if she were alive, with the same apparent indifference.

One particular Friday evening during the summer holidays, and having just completed my paper round, I was coming along the terrace on my way home, when I observed him on the next block approaching in my direction. He was dressed immaculately; no violin case this time, only a briefcase. I wondered whether I should dare to accost him in front of so many people, and the posh way he was dressed considering the obvious sight I was. He was nearly on top of me: "He can only tell me to get lost," thought I. "Hellow, Sir, remember me? Yer invited me t'cum agen t'one of yer hoose concerts."

He peered down at me, a little amused, stroking his chin with his long tapered fingers, then he smiled broadly, that contented smile of his. "Of course I remember, sir," replied he, "Then you must explain

140

your absence, did you not after all enjoy my musical repertoire?"

Whatever he meant by repertoire, I did not wish to appear ignorant. "Oh, it was smashin', mister, I've thought about it al'this time, but every Saturday I've called yer were oot," I replied.

Some of the passers-by hesitated a little, rather awed, I believe, at the spectacle of the posh-dresser, and the shabbily dressed kid, obviously enjoying a tête-à-tête.

"Do you know where I am off to now?" said he, still smiling happily, "To indulge in a musical evening away from home, and I know I shall thoroughly enjoy myself. Well, what do you think of that'hm?"

I felt envious, and would have given the world to accompany him on such an occasion. "Am gannin' to be a singer when I grow up," said I, "Everybody in oor lane tells me I can sing the 'Donkey's Serenade' better than Allan Jones."

His lips parted in a show of amazement: "My dear sir, you are a singer? Wonderful, then certainly you must come again to hear my music, and, yes, you will sing. How about that, h-m."

As he appeared keen to move on, I asked him when I should call?

"How about tomorrow, I have my dear lady friend visiting me, she plays the violin too, you know. So what about tomorrow two o'clock sharp, does that suit you?"

"Yes, sir, that's all right, I'll be there, an'I can sing other songs too."

He patted me on the head. "I can see your repertoire is unlimited also. Well, until tomorrow, I bid you good evening — oh, bring me some of your firewood along."

Off he strolled along the terrace in the direction of Benwell Village; like myself, he could step out some.

When I arrived home, everyone was sitting around the table, my father was busy cutting thick slices of bread. "Finished your papers, son?" said he. "Yes, da," I replied, unable to find a vacant space at the table, "Da — what does rep-it-wa mean?"

He went on cutting bread, directing an amusing glance at me: "Repertoire, son, it means the stock of pieces that a musician has at his finger tips. So just wash your finger tips, then sit down on the fender and I will give you your tea."

"The daft bugger," thought I, a little annoyed, "pieces at his fingertips!" I was as much wiser then, than when the Professor had first uttered the word.

The next day after lunch. I had a tussle with my conscience of whether I ought to go to the wedding hoy-oots, and earn some quick money, or go to the Professor's, with a sack of wood, and enjoy the music?

I decided on the latter, so bribing my brother John with a penny, for him to help my mother to carry the afternoon shopping, I left the house by way of the front stairs for sure enough, if I went the back way one of my pals would follow me.

On arriving there I rang the bell, and within seconds I heard the sound of the music as the inner door was opened.

142

"My dear fellow, pleased to see you, come along inside you know your way, take the firewood direct to the scullery."

I entered the living room as the record was coming to a halt, and a lady aged about forty, was standing beside the gramophone ready to lift up the sound box arm. Her appearance reminded me of a school teacher; though in looks she was plain, nevertheless, she possessed a nice pleasant face, which was just as effective as being pretty, and her eyes were lively and friendly. I assumed she too must share the same love of music, and of life in general, as the host. Her brown hair was brushed back then arranged like a cottage loaf on top and secured with a couple of tortoiseshell combs. Her tweed skirt, the same colour as her hair, was as thick as a blanket; her boots interested me, they had soft leather uppers, laced up to her calfs. Everything about her pleasant appearance displayed good taste; like the Professor's, I thought; and I assumed, if they were short of anything it was not money.

I placed the sack in the scullery and returned as she was turning the record over, and he entered the room. "Ah, Violet," said he, "This is the young man I was telling you about, and he's a singer!"

She held out a hand towards me, and I took it with pleasure, shaking it gently. The manners of the house certainly impressed me. "How delightful — I'm awfully pleased to meet you. Do you play any musical instrument at all?" she inquired.

"No, Miss. But me da can play th'fiddle, th'banjo, th'piano accordion, an'th'mouth organ; but he had t'sell them t'buy food."

She smiled at my remarks, time the Professor placed a chair next to the gramophone. "Now then, sir," said he, apparently eager to get started with the music, "First of all, can you operate a gramophone?"

"Yes, sir, I can put a record on an'off, we used t'hav'a gramophone in oor hoose."

"Good, then you are in charge of the orchestra," said he.

Violet sat down near the fireplace, took up her violin and bow and began tuning up. From off the bookcase he picked up a baton: "Now then, my young man, let us get to work and remember during the musical recital silence is golden. I will tap three times on the edge of the table with my baton, at the third tap place the sound box on to the record."

He held his baton above his head as a signal, then once-twice-three times, and I placed the sound box on to the record with perfect accuracy.

Violet began playing her fiddle as the first note of music beamed from the record, and the Professor, also on his mark, commenced his conducting. The music was similar to that of the last occasion; for me, it was an exciting music; the rhythm of which began to effect my senses in a strange fashion, somehow my imagination became alert with mental pictures that the music was recording to my soul.

I kept glancing from one to the other, and both appeared momentarily out of this world. The room was snug, and secure, and I wished then that all my life could be as pleasant as that moment.

The record came to an end, I stood up and lifted the sound box up from off the record and placed it upon its rest, and voluntarily began clapping my hands, much to the delight of them both.

The Professor was in a most delightful mood; mopping his brow with his red silk handkerchief. "Wonderful, beautiful, your playing, my dear Violet, is becoming smoother with every note you make. And you, sir, you attended to the orchestra like a maestro himself. That music you just heard was composed by Chopin. Do you like him?"

I was baffled at the sound of the odd names he rolled off his tongue, My-stro, and Show-pan; no wonder I had decided in my mind to nickname him as the Professor.

"Av niver heard music like that before — exceptin'here," I replied, "But it's gud, an'when I grow up am gannin't'buy records like that."

He took the record off the turntable, polished it with a cloth, placed it into its cover, then placed another one on. "Now then," said he, "The music you are about to hear was composed by a gentleman named Handel. So stand up, be ready to attend to the orchestra."

Moving back again to the far end of the table facing the gramophone he once more picked up his baton, as Violet began tuning up.

We went through three records both sides; what a musical appetite he had; the sweat was streaming from off his brow into his eyes, but it never restrained his efforts on the contrary, it urged him on to even more conducting. Finally, he decided it was time that my voice was auditioned. "Now then, sir, what are you going to sing for us; anything but the Donkey's Serenade, will be appreciated."

Normally I am self-conscious in the company of strangers; excepting, on the rare occasions when I meet someone whom I feel instantly at ease with; and at my first meeting with the Professor, I was able to shed all my usual inhibitions, for being in his company was as relaxing as being with anyone of my pals; and Violet was cast in his kind of mould. Therefore, when he suggested my singing a song, I did not feel at all embarrassed. However, he obviously had no time for listening to the Donkey's Serenade, and regretfully I knew the words of very few songs. But one did come to my mind, a favourite of mine, I felt sure they would both like my choice: "How aboot th'Holy City, sir?" I suggested. He raised both arms above his head in a show of approval: "Excellent, wonderful. Violet will accompany you on the violin. Now then, my good man, what key?"

I looked at him in amazement then glanced towards Violet. She fortunately grasped my predicament instantly, and explained to him.

"Ah, I see," he remarked, "You don't follow my meaning, well now, you begin singing and Violet will join in with the music."

As I sang I observed they were listening to me with the same far-away look of contentment, as when they were playing at concert-making.

146

When I finished my number they applauded so well and so sincerely, that a lump came into my throat, and for once it was not caused through hunger. Violet, lay down her violin, and both of them came up to me and made quite a fuss of me; I was not used to such pampering, but I felt good.

"Sir," said the Professor, "I most strongly advise you to join some choir, have your voice thoroughly trained, for I assure you, and I feel confident Violet will join me in saying," he looked at her for confirmation, and she nodded her head in acquiescence, "that you have the qualities that will make you someday a good tenor."

"Shall I put the kettle on, dear?" inquired Violet to him.

"Yes, of course, Violet, let us have tea before we say good-bye to our young Caruso."

They were certainly a delightful and generous couple. Time she was in the scullery busy with the tea preparations, he began looking up some sheet music, humming all the while to himself, and moving his free hand about as though he was still conducting.

"Do yer ever conduct real bands, sir?" I inquired. He appeared to ponder over my question for a while.

"I should have loved to have taken music up as a career. I had a good musical background when I was young; but unfortunately, my mother became an invalid, my father died later, I think due to the strain of looking after mother, and by the time she passed on, well, it was too late." The shadow left his face, and he smiled again. "Life is not wasted, I still have my music

147

to enjoy, and I practice, for practice makes for perfection, sir."

Violet came in with the silver tea tray, and the Professor went into another room and returned with another chair.

I really enjoyed the way they conversed with me; they talked to and addressed me as an equal, and not as a simple child; and I could never imagine any foul language, or cursing, issuing forth from either of them. After tea, I inquired of the time, and to my sorrow it was once more time to mount my imaginary horse, and hit the trail towards the newsagents. Saturday was my late night, for after delivering the Chronicle, it would be time to go out selling the late sports specials.

They both made quite a fuss of me at the front door; and once more, another invitation to call again.

However, unknown to me at that moment, I had attended my last concert at the Professor's. Once or twice I paid a call and always found him absent from home. Then one day I viewed the "For Sale" notice affixed to his garden gate; I felt as though I had lost two good pals.

Wherever they went to, I felt confident they would not only be entertaining themselves but delighting others with their music, and their old-world manners; they were wholesome company.

CHAPTER
ELEVEN

Paddy's Market

During my childhood, in the late 1920s, and the '30s, quite a fair section of the working classes had no alternative when seeking a change of clothing, footwear, or household goods, but to resort to a visit to one of the many second-hand shops, that could be found in most parts of Newcastle; or perhaps pay a visit to Paddy's Market, on a Saturday morning, down on the quayside. Many a boy and girl then, grew up into an adult state, before they were ever in a position to shop around the big stores, and purchase their first suit; or costume; or pair of shoes; even then, that would depend on whether one was employed. Indeed on the subject of footwear, I know by personal experience, and not only relating to myself, or of my brothers and sisters; but to many others, whose feet were permanently retarded, or deformed to some degree, due solely to having been compelled to don footwear that was either too small, or too large, during the formative years. Sore feet, and rickets, were but two of the maladies that afflicted a large number of children during those years; both arising from the same cause, poverty. There can be no doubt where the popular haven of second-hand shops in Newcastle was situated! During my childhood, there were nearly as many second-hand shops on Scotswood Road, that long-long-road that leads to Blaydon, as there were pubs; and it took a learned man to count the latter, especially so, if that learned man had sunk a jar or two of bass first. So my Aunt Dolly's shop was situated on the right road as far as the second-hand business in clothing was concerned.

Although she never employed anyone, apart from her daughter helping out, she nevertheless kept to proper trade union shop hours, closing about five every day, excepting on a Wednesday, when she closed for the weekly customary half day.

My Aunt Dolly was one of the hardest working women I've ever set eyes upon; she came from a hard working family, and her sister, my mother was of the same kind of mettle; and they got little thanks from anyone, only put upon.

Usually on a Monday morning, my aunt would set off from the shop at an early hour, and walk for miles around Jesmond, South Gosforth, and High Heaton, visiting her regular contacts, well-to-do people, who always reserved their good cast-offs, for her. And she was well liked and respected by these people. She always took with her a large counterpane in which to secure any article of clothing, shoes, or handbags, that may be given to her. If any of the ladies of the houses she visited, were ever feeling a little down at the mouth, then I assure all, she would be asked in by them to mid-morning tea or coffee; for if there was ever a woman who could dispel depression in others it was my aunt. Folklore, fortune-telling, tall stories, and humour in abundance, were among her many assets; in this respect, she was a chip off the old block, in reference to my maternal grandmother!

One day, remaining from school to accompany her on one of those contact missions, I enjoyed one of the most amusing and memorable days of my life. In one large house, we were entertained to morning tea and toast. Afterwards, my aunt, at the lady's request, began to read her cup.

I soon found myself struggling to prevent breaking into wild fits of laughter, for I realised within a couple of minutes of the performance commencing, that my aunt was also a perfect mimic, and she was actually imitating a local fortune-teller friend of hers, who often paid her a visit in the shop. And the jargon she was delivering to this innocent looking woman, was the same harmless nonsense word-for-word, that this friend of hers, repeated to my aunt, usually in exchange for a mug of tea, or an old pair of shoes, or hat.

With the counterpane absolutely bulging with first-class bargains for her shop, and for Paddy's market, we finally boarded the Scotswood tram. Indeed, as it took both of us struggling to manoeuvre the huge bundle on to the tram and into the downstairs compartment, I was at a loss as to why the Conductor had not ordered us off, until I heard him addressing my aunt by her Christian name in ever such a friendly manner. I gathered from their exchanges that they knew each other solely to meeting so often on the same route. It also turned out, he and his driver, were two of my aunt's "mobile customers". By the time we had almost reached the head of Osborne Road, and before we turned onto Jesmond Road, my aunt had the counterpane open; the conductor was trying a pair of shoes on, and a lady passenger was becoming ever so amorous towards a well tailored made dress coat. Such was the power of her blarney, that she could persuade tram conductors, and passengers, to try on for size, coats, waistcoats, pullovers, hats and footwear; though never trousers, skirts, or underwear; there was obviously a limit to her sales pressure!

I reckoned the only free time my aunt had to call her own was on a Sunday, after having cooked lunch. My Uncle Charley, her husband, although a harmless sort of man, he was not much of a help to her. Sitting in his favourite pub all morning taking bets, and consuming gills of Bass, was his main contribution towards the advancement of society. He drank according to the state of the racing business; the more losers among the punters, the more commission he would receive, and so the more gills of ale he put out of sight.

His indifference to the second-hand business must have been trying at times for my aunt. I think the gentleman's life was more to his taste; and he would have no more pulled a barrow to Paddy's market, than he would have taken up lion taming.

All the graft that was ever done in the family to help in making ends meet, was performed by my aunt and her daughter.

My Aunt Dolly, never missed a Saturday morning at Paddy's market, from the day she opened her business, to the day she retired, through old age! One night, just before I climbed into the double bed, my mother inquired of me whether I would assist my aunt on to the quayside with her barrow? "Do yer mean watch th'shop, time she goes on to th'quayside?" I replied, having done that before.

"No, hinny, help her with the barrow down to Paddy's market. Her daughter, your cousin, is going to watch the shop," said my mother.

I replied eagerly in the affirmative. I had never been to the market before, and my curiosity was certainly roused. I climbed into bed, and shoved my brother further over towards the wall; he was for ever attempting to grab more bed space than he was entitled to, especially my allotted plot.

"Don't forget, son, as soon as you finish delivering your papers, go straight on to your Aunt Dolly's." She gave me a halfpenny for the tram fare.

"Right-oh, ma. Mind you, it's Saturday, yer know, I git paid this mornin'," said I. My mother nodded, she was trying hard to finish a cup of tea before the rest of the family woke up.

"Your brother John will come and collect your pay, hinny, so get straight down the bank and catch a tram."

I glanced at the bed where three of my younger brothers were fast asleep; probably dreaming about Tom Mix, or Ken Maynard, chasing outlaws through Arizona; the lucky buggers. My father had just left the house on some business; he never told anyone where he was going: "I'll be back later," was all you ever got out of him.

"Why don't yer git John up now, Ma? He'll have t'gan for th'owld breed, if am gannin'on th'quayside with th'rags."

My mothers eyes beamed with annoyance. "Don't let yer aunt hear you describe her cast-off clothing as rags. You know she gets all her things from money people."

"Well, they're second-hand things, they're not like th'things yer can buy at Jackson's th'tailors, are they?" I insisted.

There was no further comment from my mother, so I left the house.

Going down the street at such an early hour in the mornings I was often accosted three or four times by neighbours, inquiring of the correct time. Why any of them wished to be informed of the time at all puzzled me, because none of them concerned were employed, nor were likely to be, until the next great war came along. I was of the conviction, that if everyone in Newcastle were suddenly to be found work, the alarm clock manufacturers would make a fortune. Sunday morning, for some unknown reason, I never got inquiries about the correct time, usually it was: "Have yer got a match, hinny, for th'gas stove?" What would I be doing with matches? A confirmed non-smoker.

Down on the terrace, the fruit and hardware merchants were beginning to erect their stalls out on the foot walk; Saturday was the only day they took this liberty.

There was no tramcar approaching in my direction, so smacking my bottom and pretending to be Tim McCoy on his horse, I galloped off towards Pendower greeting Mrs. Race, the fruitier, as I passed her shop. When I arrived at the newsagents, my boss was just taking in the bundles of newspapers, and it was six forty-five, according to the nearby Parish church clock. He was another who worshipped his bed in the mornings, instead of retiring a little earlier at night.

When I arrived back at the shop, my brother John was waiting outside. On receiving my pay, I passed it over to him, and I stood and watched him walk straight over to the opposite tram stop. I called to him. "Hey John, why don't yer walk? It's only three stops."

"Me Muther says I've got t'catch th'tram, so shut up, an'git t'th'rag shop," replied he, indignantly.

What a liberty, thought I, as I walked away. When I arrived at the Parish cemetery, the gates were still closed, so climbing over the wall, I ran to the far end, over the far wall, and down the bank to Scotswood Road. When the tram came, I observed the downstairs was full, on climbing the stairs, all I could make out in the top deck compartment through the thick shroud of tobacco smoke, were dim-round shaped objects, each with a cloth cap perched on top. I made no attempt to enter, but remained outside on the end part of the deck usually known as the windy seat; though well sought after during hot weather.

At the third stop the conductor came upstairs, when he entered the smokey compartment, he made no attempt to open any of the windows, and several of the occupants sounded as though they were coughing their lungs to shreds; I can only assume that he too was an addict, and therefore unaffected or unconcerned with the pollution.

The barrow, was practically loaded up with merchandise by the time I arrived at the shop. My aunt put on her coat, and made to get in between the cart shafts, but I would not hear tell of it. "I'll pull th' barrow, Aunt Doll', I'm strong." So she remained at the back of the cart, pushing and holding back, whenever circumstances demanded it.

As we passed the cattle market, she directed me to turn right, then first left towards Forth Bank, which would lead us on to the quayside, and also avoid the busy traffic at the Central Station.

The lane leading us directly on to the quay was pretty narrow, with very old buildings situated along either side. Those on the right hand side facing on to the Tyne, were mostly warehouses; and the buildings on the left side, had been in their time, shops and houses, above them stood the Keep of the Castle.

"There must have been a lot of smugglers aboot here in th'olden days, Aunty," I called out loudly to enable my voice to be heard above the din of the cart wheels over the cobble stones.

"There's still a few queer buggers aboot noo, so don't stop t'talk to anyone, bonny lad," replied she, shoving the barrow suddenly, as though I wasn't going fast enough.

As we arrived on the quayside, the clock of the church steeple situated on the other side of the river, chimed half past eight. I observed a large merchant ship berthed alongside the quayside, and a number of seamen were coming ashore down the gangplank, all wearing big yellow clogs on their feet. That was the first time I had witnessed footgear made solely of wood. "Are they gannin't'do a clog dance in them wooden shoes, aunty?" I called out.

"Don't shout, bonny lad," replied she, looking a little concerned, "They're Dutchmen, but th'buggers may understand Inglish, al'these foreigners are a funny lot."

They certainly dress funny, thought I. Their trousers were blown out and appearing like coloured balloons. My aunt directed me to pull up Milk Street. She lifted the large bundle down on to the ground, opened it, and arranged the suits, coats, dresses, and underwear, in neat order; leaving the footwear on the barrow. "Keep an eye on th'shoes, Thomas," she confided in me, "There's sum clever people cums doon here, who don't believe in partin'with money!"

Dealers were still arriving from all directions, mainly from the direction of City Road, and Byker. Some with handcarts, others with suitcases, and old prams, one man had a horse and cart. Soon there was quite a gathering, the market was ready to commence.

My Aunt, it turned out and very early on too, had a regular clientele, who on arriving on the scene, made direct towards her pitch, and began fitting, examining, then bargaining, for her superior cast-offs.

I glanced along towards the nearest of our competitors, a small stout woman; then I cast my gaze to wander over her merchandise, and I seriously wondered how she had the nerve to set up shop? I was never well dressed at the best of times, but I reckoned,

I would have to be dressing up for Guy Fawkes night, to wear some of the rags she was hoping to sell.

Although I was full of curiosity at this new scenic experience in my life, I was also of the instant opinion that it was really a depressing sight, for on the whole, the majority of the dealers were as shabbily dressed as the prospective customers; it was a classical example of penury, seeking some form of subsistence out of distress!

All I was expected to do was to keep both eyes glued on to the stock, and ensure that no absent minded character left the scene of my aunt's stall with a magnificent bargain, without having first paid for it. Three pretty young ladies, aged — I think about twenty, or near-so, began holding up skirts, then dresses, to their persons, judging for size and effect; time the usual male idlers, who always turn up on such occasions, were doing their utmost verbally, to encourage the ladies to try the garments on, and provide a partial strip-tease show for their benefit; but my aunt, was one too many for such comics, and they soon moved on. I could not but think that such young ladies ought to be in a solvent position to be able to shop around in the big stores up town, and not having to frequent second-hand shops and markets; despite the garments on my aunt's stall having once been owned by rich people, living in large houses, and over-employing underpaid servants.

A man approached from an alleyway, having around him a sandwich board. On the front of the board were the words: "Repent For The Day Of Judgement

Draweth Nigh." And on the back of it, "Repent Your Sins — Before It Is Too Late." What struck me about him was he possessed the most depressing and heartbroken countenance in sight; and believe me, there were plenty of competitive examples about; the poor devils.

"Who's he workin'for, Aunt Doll?" I inquired, rather curious at the man's apparent distress.

"Take nee notice of him, bonny lad, he's more t'pity. He lives in th'Salvation Army, an'even they can't put up with his sermons."

He came walking alongside the scattered chain of make-shift stalls, chanting in a high pitched squeaky voice his message of prospective doom. "Repent ye sinners before it's too late."

I considered it an odd rendezvous for such as himself to appear, and I wondered whether he was carrying out a vendetta against the second-hand merchants? Though to judge by his own dress, it was most highly improbable. He was either short sighted, or just plain spiteful, for he suddenly came in too close, and walked over some clothing belonging to the small fat woman next to my aunt's stall; and on he walked without even uttering an apology.

"Here, yer waster, you cum back here agen — an'I'll kick yer arse for yer, yer stupid get, go on — git back t'th' 'Sally' with yer preachin'."

The preacher of doom, never bothered to turn round, and I looked eagerly towards the fat woman, hoping she was going to go after him, and set about him; her face was scarlet through temper.

159

"He's not taken any notice of yer, Missis," said I, hoping to encourage her. She clenched her right hand and produced a fist that Jack Dempsey, would have been proud of. "He'll tak'note of this sunk in his chops if he cums back here, th'religious loon-atick. Did yer see 'im stampin' reet on that gud soot?"

The suit in question, which lay on the ground, and which by rights was the fit place for it, had obviously seen far more service than was intended. Aunt Doll beckoned on me with her eyes, and when I came close up to her, she whispered, "Listen, bonny lad, divint encourage Bella, once she starts shoutin' iveryone from as far as Daisy Hill will be alerted." She gave me twopence, and pointed in the direction of the café: "Nip to the cafe: an'git yourself a cup of tea an'a t'cake."

The café was situated on the corner of Trinity Chare; and it occupied. a part of the ground floor of a very old building, next to it was a pub which was frequented by the dockers and seamen.

Entering the cafe I got myself served then moved into the back room. At one table sat a group of the foreign seamen, who appeared to be enveloped in a pocket of fog, for each of them were smoking, as though their very existence depended on it. At another table sat four women, all of them second-hand dealers; one of them, who has her hair smothered in metal curling pins, invited me to their table, and I sat down at the only vacant space facing her. "Are you Dolly's lad?" she inquired before I could get started on my snack.

160

"No, Missis," guessing instantly, why she had invited me to the table. "She's me aunt, an'I am only helpin'her," and that is all your going to get to know, said I to myself.

"Where does yer Aunt git al'her stuff from, hinny?" asked the same woman. At that moment, the "End of the World" merchant entered the room, a mug of tea in one hand, and his sandwich board in the other which he placed and sat at the only remaining table, alongside two dossers. The distraction caused by his entry, enabled me to devour my teacake; but before the woman in the hair pins, could recommence her inquisition, I decided to ask a question. "Who employs that man t'gan around with that board aroond his neck?" I directed my inquiry to the woman sitting next to me. "Aye — I suppose he's got nothin'better t'do, hinny," replied she.

As I expected, the inquisitive woman volunteered information on the subject. "Av heard that sum rich man livin'in Sooth Gosforth pays him a poond a week t'do it, an'of course he gits his dole into th'bargain, 'cause nee one can prove he gits paid for it; an'I hear this rich bugger dosn't want anyone t'know his bissness."

This explanation appeared to satisfy the other three women at the table; even the two large tabby cats sitting nearby looking up at us as though listening in to the conversation, appeared to be taken in by her rather dubious information.

"I suppose this rich man is a religious lunatic too," suggested the woman at the far end of the table on my

161

side, who was wearing on her head what appeared to be a leek-pudding cloth.

I was about to commence on my mug of tea, when suddenly I felt the atmosphere in the room change dramatically, silence stole over the company; even the two dossers ceased rambling over the number of lodging houses they had kipped in, in their time. I turned my head sideways towards the entrance of the room; at that instance the buzz of conversation began slowly to grind once more. A young lady stood in the entrance, a cup of tea in one hand and a cigarette in the other. She was dressed in a dazzling bright red costume which matched the colour of her hair, and a gorgeously coloured blouse. She was wearing black high heeled shoes, and her legs — they appeared to be remarkably long and ever so shapely. I could not conceal my admiration of her, and she smiled at me, a beautiful elder sister smile; then she cast her gaze upon the women at my table, who could not conceal the mixture of envy and contempt in their eyes; she scanned each of their faces with a searching look, and in her own eyes at that moment, could be read: "Yes, I am pretty, and smart, you ugly cantankerous ducklings, and I know what you all are thinking of me!"

My word, she was pretty too, I wondered what on earth had decided her to enter this down-at-heel teashop. The building, I had heard, was about 400 years old, and most probably had in its early days, catered for roughnecks, footpads, and probably river smugglers; whether its interior had ever been graced by the presence of such a young beautiful damsel, as she was, I would personally doubt it.

The taller of the seamen stood up, and beckoned on her to join their table; greeting his gesture with a sweet smile she willingly obliged.

I discreetly followed her with my eyes; and when she raised a leg to manoeuvre the form, to sit beside him, her skirt involuntary crept up to the top of her thigh, revealing stocking top, and milk-white flesh. I was delighted at the sight; but to judge by the faces of the four women sitting with me, who also had watched her every move, they were undeniably incensed. "The brazen huzzy," muttered the one next to me, "Luk at her skirt, it's reet up t'her bottom, an'if she hooks it any tighter it will split."

"She can smell a room full of seamen from as far as Jesmond," remarked the woman with the leek pudding cloth secured on her head.

The one with the hair curlers so prominent upon her head, was, it soon appeared not to be denied her usual contribution to the numerous criticisms that were being made against the young redhead. "Well, I hear tell, that she is well ed-ucated, an'one man who knows her very well — th'dirty bugger that he is; he told me, her father is sum big nob doon Sooth," As usual her remarks appeared to satisfy the other three; unless they were afraid to contradict her. I drank off my tea, determined to be away from the gossips; as I left, the cats followed me out; I reckoned they too had heard all they could put up with.

On my way back to the market I observed a crowd, mostly men, gathering around a man, who was on one knee, chalking names and numbers on the ground. Being curious as usual, I pushed my way into the inner circle. Having completed his chalking exercise, the man stood up, very erect like an old soldier. He was of average height, and slim built. The suit he was wearing, though well worn and over pressed, had the appearance of being of good quality a hell-ava long time ago. I pondered as to whether he had purchased it then, from my Aunt. His black patent leather shoes, well, if he polished them much more, he would end up rubbing his socks to shreds. On his head was a black bowler, which like his suit, was simply begging to be pensioned off. There was a small hole in its crown, though large enough for a tuft of steel grey hair to be protruding, the whole reminded me of an old cooking pot that had been discarded on some tip, with weeds forcing their way through. His large moustache with the ends tapering to fine points, gave him a kind of military appearance. I naturally assumed, that if the inquisitive woman with the hair curlers, and who was still in the cafe, was to set eyes upon this character, she would no doubt confide in her cronies confidentially of course, that this smart looking con man, was no other than the outcast brother of the Duke of Northumberland. However, I must admit his face had about it quite a proud and dignified look; the probable remains of much better days, unless of course, I had due to my youth, underestimated his obvious unique abilities as a character actor. Placing his hands on his hips, and

164

giving a sort of casual glance around his audience, he took a deep breath, then in a voice so robust, and commanding, which would on any racecourse, make him the envy of every tipster in sight, he began his introduction.

"My friends, yesterday I was at Hexham races. Today, I ought to have been at Pontefract!" He paused again, and twirled the ends of his moustache, an exercise which he appeared to enjoy. "But, my friends," he began talking again in that beautiful rich fruity voice of his. "I had the good fortune to bump into Lord Roseberry, an old friend of mine.

"'Ah — Captain Baines,' said he, 'Why my good fellow, I have not set eyes upon you since Ascot, last year, it was last year, wasn't it? Of course it was. You must come and lunch with me and my trainer.'" Another twirl of the moustache. "So, my friends, off we went, the three of us, Lord Roseberry, his trainer, and your old friend Captain Baines. And I don't have to repeat that every man on this quayside knows of the integrity of Captain Baines, my word is my bond. Well, we had lunch at the Station Hotel, Hexham; and as a result, of no mean importance to myself, as well as my many friends, a number of whom I recognise this morning, I was given certain information which I deemed too good to keep to myself. So, my friends, I am here this morning to share with you the knowledge that has been passed on to me. My friends, I have the winners of the first four races at Pontefract today."

I was fascinated with his story and the confident way he was relating it; his deliberate pauses, the individual glance to certain members of his audience, who eagerly responded with a nod of the head, being greatly flattered on his singling them out for such personal attention. And the continuous twitching of his moustache, which at times appeared as though it was going to set off in motion like a plane propellor.

From out of his inside jacket pocket, he brought out a package of small slips of folded note paper, upon which, he claimed were written the winners of the first four races at Pontefract. Before disclosing the price of this information, he pointed down on to the ground, to the facts and figures, which he had chalked out, previous to opening his meeting.

"As you all can see, last Sunday morning, which is my usual day for coming down on to the quay; I forecast five winners out of six, and the sixth one came in third. I defy any tipster, my friends, to beat that record. Furthermore, I am willing to pay fifty pounds, to any man here, who can name me any tipster who has such a successive run of winners as Captain Baines. Well, my friends, I have said all I intend saying this morning, anyone who wishes to purchase my information, it will cost them threepence."

And surprisingly enough, those at the back of his audience began rudely pushing their way into the inner circle in their haste to purchase his slips of paper. "What an easy way to earn money," thought I! There and then. I disowned my previous intentions of becoming a tenor, or a Blacksmith, when I grew up. Instead I would become a star tipster; and I too would seek to have lunch with some titled horse owner, and trainer, and obtain direct information on racehorses, who were destined at some particular meeting to be first past-the-post. But I would present my information in a more stylish manner in a sealed envelope, and thus increase my fee to a shilling. For I was convinced there would still be sufficient punters around who would sample anything, providing it came from one who could talk nonsense in a professional and dignified manner.

Going up Milk Street, I gazed awhile at one or two of the stalls; one in particular, run by a woman, who had a boy and girl with her, both of whom I guessed were about my own age; she was doing her utmost to persuade a potential customer, also a woman, to purchase a large faded bedspread which she was examining. The time this was taking place, a girl aged about fourteen, who it appeared was the daughter of the potential customer, was sitting on the parapet of the railings, the dealer's own girl was on her knees fitting a reasonable looking pair of patent leather shoes to her feet. They appeared to fit perfectly, for she stood up, traces of joy and anxiety showing in her eyes, imploring her mother to buy them for her. I could have been mistaken, but I felt sure I detected a glimpse of disappointment steal over the face of the dealer's own daughter. She sensed I was interesting myself in her apparent feelings, for she immediately turned her back on me, and busied herself with the pretence of rearranging an old fur coat that was resting on the railings.

I glanced down at her own footwear, like my own, and her brothers, and their mothers, they were holding together through sheer necessity! But, as my father often remarked, "In hard times, only fools worry about their dress, while their stomachs are empty and crying out to be filled." When I got back to my aunt, she was in the best of moods, and I saw by the declining stock, that she was doing very well.

A foreign seaman came up to her stall, and picked up a smart evening dress coat. He tried it on and it was a perfect fit. My aunt immediately got to work on him. Informing him, that the previous owner of the coat, had been no other than one of the ex-Lord Mayors of the city. She bid him turn around slowly all the time praising the coats qualities, the cut, and the colour; and then, what a fine figure of a man he was, and how the coat appeared as though it had been specially tailored for him. And of course she pointed out, that the garment had been made by one of the most expensive tailors in Britain, Moss Brothers.

What a vain man he appeared to be, swallowing the old blarney about his fine figure, and his obvious good taste. There was no self-consciousness about him, he delighted in the attention being bestowed upon him, his antics were more in the fashion of a model, than that of an ordinary potential customer. Time my aunt was putting on the sales pressure in regards to the seaman, she began laying on the syrup, for the benefit of a small middle-aged lady who had picked up a smart pair of blue dress shoes from off the cart to admire. "You ought to snap them up, hinny, at five shillings. Only a few weeks ago they were worn for the last time by one of the richest women in Newcastle, at a ball in th'Old

Assembly Rooms." My aunt was never backward in stretching a point or two when she deemed it necessary; and I suppose in business it is nearly always so. The lady was in the act of replacing them on to the barrow, after listening to such biographic details apparently a little afraid to consider purchasing such pedigree footwear.

"Don't do that, hinny," interposed my aunt, "You'll regret it for th' rest of yer life. They cost aboot seven guineas a pair in Paris."

I wondered what kind of people they were who could afford to cast-off such serviceable gear; although I had been inside some of the houses of my aunt's benefactors, I remained in the dark as regarding the source of their wealth; undoubtedly they had to be very well-off, for to afford to be so frivolous in their dress tastes, and thus be able to give away such good quality merchandise. I am not here complaining of these well-heeled individuals, who lived in such large houses having a dozen rooms or more, all of which would no doubt be heated when required, by coal fires, which in turn, would require an abundance of firewood! On the contrary, I deeply regretted living so far outside their boundaries, and the obvious business potential of selling firewood: not to mention the cast-off clothing and footwear I would have scored for.

My aunt decided to bring back the seaman from out of the clouds: "Fifteen shillings, bonny lad."

He replied in broken English. "Madame, I beg of you, please to understand, I am only deck seaman. I likes the coat that once belongs to Lord Mayor, but I say to you, please, ten shillings?"

My aunt was impressed; not with his offer, but with his good simple approach. "Alreet, bonny lad, for you ten shillin's."

He took out a purse from his back trouser pocket, taking out a ten shilling note he handed it to her, bowed in the continental manner, then walked off still wearing the dress coat. Next to be dealt with was the lady, who immediately closed the deal, and she too, went off in a most contented manner, with the dress shoes that were supposed to have cost seven guineas in Paris. Such was the crazy world of commerce, and economics, as far as my Aunt's stall was concerned, at Paddy's Market.

I observed the racing tipster coming up the road, and I brought my aunt's attention to his progress. "He must be an important bloke, Aunty, he had lunch yesterday with Lord Roseberry, in Hexham."

But she only smiled, in her good natured fashion. "Don't believe it, bonny lad, if he had any lunch at al'yesterday, it would be in th'pie-and-chip shop behind th'Gaiety Music Hall."

The church clock in the distance began chiming eleven o'clock. "Keep an eye on th'things, bonny lad," said my aunt, "I'll be back in a jiffy." I observed her progress from the stall to the pub. But back in a jiffy she was, bringing with her a pint of beer. "Is that Bass, Aunty?" I inquired, assuming she drank the same sort of wallop as me Uncle Charley. Before she answered me, she took a good swig of her beer, and in one go drained the glass of half its contents. "No, hinny, it's Best Scotch. Bass is too strong for yer aunt."

I wondered who she thought she was kidding, I knew she liked a drop of the hard stuff whenever she could afford it, so I considered Bass would be no problem. "Is beer gud for yer, Aunty?"

Placing the glass to her lips once more, she drained the remainder of the beer, then began licking the froth remaining from off the top of the glass as though she was indulging in an ice-cream cornet; satisfaction and contentment gleaming in her eyes. "No, bonny lad," she finally replied. "Beer is bad for iveryone, I would close al'the' pubs doon if I had my way."

"Then why do yer drink beer then if it's bad for yer?" I insisted, determined to get at the bottom of the issue.

"'Cause am thirsty, silly lad," replied she in a serious tone.

I decided not to question the matter any further, but I remained unsatisfied with her reply. If she was thirsty, she could drink tea in the cafe down the road, and I reckoned it was every bit as strong as any Best Scotch, that was ever brewed; and cheaper too.

A man carrying a black briefcase came up to the cart. I was confident he was a man, although his hair style, and mode of dress, were strikingly feminine. He was dressed in a dark blazer, a dark woollen skirt, a black silk blouse with a brooch shaped like a woman's head, secured to the throat, and on his feet, strong walking shoes and thick woollen stockings that reached to just above the knees, and the odour of perfume was strong upon him. Picking up a pair of black dance

171

shoes from off the barrow, he began admiring them. "What beautiful shoes to go dancing in," said he, in a voice every bit as feminine as his appearance, it was light, and musical; I could not place his dialect, but one thing was certain, he was not a Geordie. "How much will you take for these shoes, dear? Not too much, I hope." He gave a brief girlish giggle, and winked at my aunt. She did not appear to know him, which I found rather surprising, for I had formed the opinion that morning that she knew all the characters that frequented Paddy's market. "Those shoes in yer hand, hinny, have glided over sum of the best ballrooms in Europe," remarked my aunt, whom I gathered was doing her utmost to size him up; possibly wondering, how much he could afford to scoff-up; but his countenance was impenetrable. "Seven an'six to you, hinny," she finally uttered.

I was confident that particular sum, was a favourite of her's, for it had passed her lips quite a few times that morning.

"Oh — don't be a spoilsport, darling," replied he, a roguish twinkle in his eyes, "That's too much."

She paused, as though deciding whether she could allow any reduction, from that quoted, for such good quality shoes; but no doubt, it was the usual professional business pause!

"Al'reet, hinny, am giving them away, five bob to you."

From out of his briefcase he brought a purse, made of silk or satin, and was covered all over with tiny coloured beads. He paid my aunt with two half-crowns, placed the shoes into his case, and blowing a kiss in our direction, walked away down towards the quay.

"What does he dress up in woman's clothes for, Aunt Dolly?" I inquired.

"Well, bonny lad, just remember th'world's full of queer buggers, but they're al'sumbody's bairns," she replied.

So we prepared for our journey back to the family wardrobe. I pulled over to the kerbside outside the cafe, time my aunt returned the pint glass to the pub. After a lapse of time I sensed she was no doubt having it topped-up again, so I sat down on one of the cart shafts.

A small elderly woman, who was wearing a large thick shawl around her shoulders which was secured by a massive safety pin, walked slowly by; in each hand she was carrying a bulky brown paper parcel, each tied up with rough twine; and by the sound of it, she was having a hell-ava argument with herself. Her dispute was progressing like the following: "What's in yer parcels, Missis?" "Nowt for yea, they're full of bugs from North Shields, so put that in yer bloody pipe an'may it choke yer — yer nosey get, g'wan away wi'yer."

After she had advanced on a few yards past me, she placed her parcels down on to the pavement, then made her way back towards me. When she drew near, I spoke to her: "Divint worry, Missis, al'keep an eye on yer parcels for yer." And to this innocent and well intended offer of mine, she gave such a piercing shout, that everyone nearby turned quickly round facing in our direction, all of them looking at me severely, as though I was guilty of having assaulted the poor demented woman.

"Keep an eye on yer barrow, yer little waster, an off me property. Put that up yer jumper, me lad," said she. And off she went back up into Trinity Chare; to return a few moments later carrying another two shabby looking parcels, and still muttering to herself.

I sat bewildered, and watched her slow progress along the quay towards the Swing Bridge, repeating the same slow and monotonous process all the while, forward with a couple of bundles, then back again for the other two. "What a peculiar woman," thought I, "And what a peculiar way to travel."

When Aunt Dolly returned, off we rumbled along the quay. As we overtook the strange woman, my aunt called out to her. "How's life, Jessy-hinny?" The woman lifted her head as though it was an effort, and recognised my aunt. "It's you, is it, Dolly? Well, am mindin'me own bliddy bissness, an'ivery bugger ought t'do th'same. Put that on yer barrow an'pull it."

I turned my head to face my aunt behind the cart: "She's easily upset, Aunty, what's rang with her?"

"She's always like that, bonny lad. Poor soul, she wanders for miles ivery day of her life, cartin'those useless bundles around."

From that day on, I continued periodically to see that poor strange woman; right up till I was a young man, and she was still engaged in carrying her bundles around.

When I arrived back at the shop, my aunt gave me some pocket money, a meal, and two shillings for my mother; then I returned the barrow for her. I decided it was too late to attempt my firewood round. However, I was convinced the day had been well spent, despite the number of depressing sights I had witnessed, and I looked forward to my next visit.

CHAPTER
TWELVE

Saturday Night in Newcastle

In 1937 my brother John was given the pleasure of a week at the Lord Mayor's Holiday camp in Amble, during the school summer break. Ever since my own visit the year previous, I had never ceased reminiscing about it. Not only the advantage of having a week's holiday beside the sea, with good food, and a bed to myself, but the actual location of the camp itself; I had fallen in love with Amble at first sight. Unusual though it may seem coming from the then mind of a young boy, the natural uncommercial landscape of the coast-line, and the surrounding area, had appealed to me far more than had South Shields, the only other seaside I had visited up to that date.

On the second morning of my brother's absence from home, I went out early as usual to do my paper round; dressed in my regular fashion, with short trousers, shirt, jersey, and sand shoes on my feet. Little did I realise how undressed I would appear, and feel, before that day was out!

My brother Arthur had been delegated to go for the old bread.

On completing my round, and having had my thoughts on Amble all during that time, I suddenly, on coming out of the shop, and on the spur of the moment, knowing I had a penny on me, crossed over the road and boarded a tram to town. For a halfpenny I rode as far as the Grainger market. I walked straight through it, and directly in to the wholesale fruit market, where after a short while I succeeded in sponging two or three apples, and a few carrots, which I wrapped up in tissue paper.

Walking up to the Haymarket, I made a few innocent inquiries from various strangers, relating to the direction of Amble. I again boarded a tram, and with my last halfpenny rode to the terminal at Gosforth Park. Then off I set up the North Road towards my destination. I continued tramping until I reached the boundary of Plessey Woods, then sat down on the roadside to eat half of my provisions. I must have been walking another hour when I decided to chance my luck at thumbing a lift. No one appeared to take any notice of me; I was undoubtedly too young to be mistaken for a regular hitch-hiker, or a hobo, and too shabby to be mistaken for a Leprechaun. I wondered whether I ought to turn back, but still I walked on. Eventually, and I suppose out of sheer curiosity, a motorist did pull up, and surprisingly inquired where I was heading for? "Am goin'to Amble, Sir, to see me Uncle," I replied.

"You're a bit young to be travelling alone," said he, "Do your parents know about it?"

"My mother is already in Amble," said I, "An'me uncle will bring us back in his car."

He appeared dubious, but probably thought there could be truth in my remarks, for he invited me to climb in. He continued to quiz me on the journey, but I was able to ward off his suspicions; and when he dropped me off outside Amble, he wished me a good visit to my uncle.

When I arrived on the seafront. the boys from the camp were scattered all over the place, so I carefully manoeuvred my way among the sand dunes, until I was able to waylay a lad whom I recognised, and urged him to seek my brother John for me. My brother was amazed to see me, then angry, and called me a lunatic. However he agreed to smuggle me some of his lunch out in between some bread, which along with my raw carrots, made quite a satisfying meal for any wayfarer. "You had better gan yem now," said he, handing me a halfpenny, as though Newcastle was only a tram ride away. "If you're here a week, so am I," I replied, determined to stick it out, "I'll kip on the beach."

But he also was equally determined, and reminded me, that his appetite was every bit as large as my own, and that I could not expect him to feed me out of his rations. On that point I realised he was only stating a fact which I was aware of, so I asked him to grub-stake me out of his teatime meal, then I would make my way back home.

"You'll get bashed when yer git back home," he remarked, as an afterthought.

"If me da bashes me when I get back yem, I'll bugger off for good," I replied, a little annoyed at being reminded of what possibly lay in store for me. Keeping myself out of the way of any of the teachers, I lay down among the sand dunes for the afternoon.

About six o'clock that evening I was once more outside Amble, this time heading south.

Amazing though it may seem now, I walked for miles down the North Road, and every motorist I signalled to, ignored me; dusk was approaching fast, yet no one was curious or apparently interested as to why I was so far out on the highway at that time of night on my own. Darkness fell and there being no footpath I was compelled to travel on the grass verge on the side of the road; of course there were not so many cars around those days, so I was reasonably safe. Finally I came to a vicarage on the outskirts of a small village, and I immediately advanced up the driveway, and knocked on the side door. It was opened by a lady, who turned out to be the housekeeper. She looked on me with surprise, for no doubt, residing in such a small village she would realise that I did not live in the locality. On reflection, it is possible by my appearance that she thought I may have been the off-spring of some wandering Tinkers. Although it had been a warm day, the night was very cool, and I was certainly not dressed for a night march. "You could do with a coat on, young man. What is it you want?" she inquired, holding the door open only slightly.

"Can I have shelter here until t'morrow, Missis, please?" said I.

My request must have amazed her, for she opened the door wide and stood back a little. "Stay here for the night? Now then, what are you up to? Run away from home, I'll bet. Come inside the scullery awhile. Where are you from?"

"Newcastle, Missis; but I hav'nt ran away." "Alright sit down time I go and see the vicar." She closed the scullery door behind her and vanished into the front of the house.

After a lapse of about five minutes, she returned with the good man himself. I decided it would be unwise to keep to the story of visiting an uncle; so I told him the truth; and it took all my persuasion to change his mind about reporting my escapade to the Police; despite my realising that my absence from home would have already been reported to the local station. His housekeeper provided me with supper, and then I was allowed to lie on the parlour floor covered with a blanket, beside a securely guarded all night fire.

Next morning after breakfast, he provided me with my bus fare to Newcastle. I have never forgot his kind action; certainly in the spirit of a good Samaritan.

The most remarkable thing about the whole episode was, when I arrived home, and my father returned from informing the local police of my safe arrival, he did not give me the hiding I was expecting. He gave me a good stiff dressing down, then appeared to have given me up as hopeless.

Although times continued to be hard, and money forever hard to come-by, the city centre on a Saturday night, appeared to my eyes at least, to be a gay, lively and humorous place. Most people out-and-about, were well spruced up, suits and dresses, well pressed, faded shoes shining, and all wearing their best caps, and bonnets, with an occasional black dut in view; and of course, as many tappers abroad as there were spendthrifts. For weeks I had been saving twopence out of my sixpence pocket money that I received for my delivering papers, message running for neighbours, and selling firewood. Every three weeks I changed the coppers from out of my handkerchief, in exchange for a sixpenny piece, then I concealed the silver coin in the rafters in the wash house. With ten of us living in overcrowded conditions, privacy even for a few minutes was impossible, therefore I could not secrete my money in the house. And of course I had to be very careful when I was hiding my tanners in the wash house that no one saw me, for one tanner, would have purchased fifteen Woodbines, or three quarters of a pound of liquorice allsorts, or nutty bon-bons.

This particular Saturday that I am writing about, my savings amounted to three bob; so after lunch I caught a tram to the town, and made my way to the wholesale shop, and purchased a small stock of shoe laces, threads, buttons, needles and safety pins. Returning home with my goods in a cardboard box, I concealed the lot inside the wash house.

After completing my evening round, and selling my quota of evening specials, I had tea, and set about

181

improving my appearance. By six o'clock, I, too, was all spruced-up like a toff, a second-hand one, of course. Lately on account of my selling firewood on a Saturday, and thereby missing the children's afternoon matinee, I was allowed to go to the cinema on a Saturday night, first house, providing I could get someone to take me in. So I let it be known that I was off to the Adelaide cinema. Retrieving my box out of the wash house, I made my way on to the terrace. Near the Sutton Dwellings, I found Ginger sitting on the wall, he appeared worn out and miserable; and his reform school rig-out was all creased up. I could not get him to admit whether he was on official leave, or had scarpered off from the home. To judge by his condition, I would have guessed that he had been recently kipping rough. His eyes were vacant, almost devoid of life, the old fire had left them, and he was now obviously nervous as a kitten. He was fifteen now, yet I was convinced a boy of eight could have chased him out of sight; he would have been hopeless now at the wedding hoy-oots. When I had first heard of him being sent to a reform school, I had expressed the view that authority had incarcerated the wrong lad to tame. When I looked at him sitting there lost to the world, and so pathetic, my anger rose as sudden and as fierce as an eruptive volcano. There was no doubt in my mind that severe physical and mental treatment must have been used against him from the beginning; for there was no other explanation to account for his present condition, that of a permanent simpleton. What little sense I could get out of him, I learned that his keepers had sworn to beat discipline into him; they had certainly succeeded. If ever a boy had been in need of understanding, and if ever a boy had been born to be free from the child-minding system, described as elementary education, it was he. Despite his failings, he was one of the most helpful and kindest lads in the district.

The educational authorities had used their powers, in order to have him sent to a reform school, due to his playing the wag from school. Which really was ironical from my point of view, for every year that had passed I knew of local lads leaving school at fourteen, after years of continuous good attendance, and their final reward, was the choice between hanging around the back lanes, or joining the ranks of the street corner men. I bid him a sad farewell and continued on my way to the tram stop.

The tram arrived and I jumped aboard. "Downstairs, sonny," called out the conductor to me. What a bloody life, frustrated at every step. I loved to be on the top deck, especially on such a tram as this was, that had a portion of the upper deck that was open to the heavens. I loved to stand out there and pretend I was a Skipper on my ship's bridge, plodding its way through the ocean.

I got off opposite the Stoll cinema, and made my way towards the Marble bar. Davey, the paper seller was standing there as usual, calling out in a seemingly foreign language, "Cor-Gay, cor-gay," which was supposed to mean Evening Chronicle. "Why don't yer call out Evening Chronicle, Davey? That's what yer sellin'." I remarked to him.

"Hellow, Titch," said he, ignoring my criticism, "What have yer got in th'box?"

Tich, mind you. And him, fifty years old, and only a couple of inches taller than myself, when he has his cap on. "I've got tame mice in th'box," I replied, and bid him goodnight. I knew if I lingered one minute longer, he would be wanting me to take over his pitch and sell his papers, time he went into the bar to drain his earnings away.

I called into the first pub I came to in Clayton Street. Although it was only half past six business inside the bar was brisk. The big fat barman, whose left eye bore the unmistakable sign of having been in close contact with someone's fist within the last two days or so, was the first one to take notice of my presence, and as I was about to remove the lid from my box which contained my merchandise, he called out in a sharp voice: "Out of here, Nipper, or I'll put my boot up yer arse."

"Why don't yer serve th'slops yer sellin'as beer, an'leave me alone," I replied in an indignant tone. He lifted up the counter hatch and made as though he intended coming after me. I made for the door: "Hey, fat-face," I called out before leaving, "I hope someone blacks yer other eye before th'neet is oot, yer cheeky waster." Out I ran and concealed myself in a shop doorway in case he did follow me; though if he did do, I could not imagine him keeping pace with my speed.

Up the street I went, turned the corner into Newgate Street, and witnessed a large queue outside the Empire music hall. They were certainly going to have a long wait until second-house. A busker was standing at the kerbside amusing them with his accordion; so on the spur of the moment, I walked towards the crowd and began worming my way down the inner side of the queue, advertising my wares. I realised at that moment that at such times, being small could be profitable, for if the busker saw me distracting his audience, then for sure, he would be another one offering to give me the taste of boot leather. By the time I had reached the head of the queue, I had sold two and threepence worth of merchandise. Carefully concealing myself from the busker, who was now making his own collection, I slipped into the Rose and Crown, next to the music hall.

Apart from those sitting at the tables, the usual bar loungers were standing three deep, so I felt sure the bar staff would have to be raised on stilts to spot me. I began attempting to weigh up those sitting at the tables, wondering whether any of them had drank sufficient to diminish their senses a little and put them in a generous mood. A group of men sitting together, all dressed in black three piece suits, watch chains, and duts, appeared to be in a humorous mood, so I approached them.

"I'll buy a pair of shoe laces, Nipper, if yer will drink a pint of beer standing on your head with your mouth closed," remarked this chap who looked like a cheery undertaker.

"Have you any safety pins that won't fasten, hinny?" said his mate beside him, whose belly was shaking from side to side like a huge jelly, as he laughed. These two set the ball rolling, for the rest of their company

185

took their cue from them, and all of them began taking the mickey out of me. And I reckon due to them, the rest of the customers sitting at the tables ignored me. As I was moving towards the exit, a tall man entered dressed in a green suit, a new cap. and a pipe in his hand. He glanced at the box in my hand, then cast his attention on me, deliberately blocking my departure. "Do your parents know you're doing this?" he inquired in an abrupt manner. I glanced down on his well polished shoes, size ten or eleven, was my guess, and concluded he was an off duty copper.

"No, me da an'ma don't know," replied I.

"Hm, where do you live?" he asked. I felt myself becoming an object of curiosity. There was another exit nearby, but before I could make a move in that direction, a small over-dressed woman, sitting at a table behind me, must have taken in the whole situation, for she came over and placed herself deliberately between myself and my inquisitor.

"No one bought anything off you, son, you just wait on and I'll see what I can do with the stingy buggers." She took the box from me, and turned to face the tall man: "Well, darlin', do you want anythin'," she inquired holding up the box under his nose. He blinked his eyes once or twice, shrugged his shoulders, and moved over to the bar.

"What a persuasive woman," thought I, as she continued round the room, like a one woman pressgang; and I don't think I had ever seen so many people change their mind in so short a time. She was certainly a colourful looking character, and pretty well

186

dressed for the times, apart from the long fox fur she had wrapped round her shoulders, her large flowered hat was most unique; mind you I think the cosmetics were applied a little heavy, indeed besides the hat, it was her cosmetics alone that made her appear overdressed and most conspicuous.

She returned the box to me with the money inside, and I thanked her kindly. "Watch out for that man that was talking to you, son, and asking questions, he's a Policeman. And don't go into the pub across the road facing this one, because that's another one of his haunts." I thanked her again for the tip-off; she had her heart in the right place, good woman.

I felt it a great pity that her mother had not given her a few tips on how to dress fashionable, both in respects of the body and the face, for underneath the paint she was undoubtedly a nice looking woman.

Though however one looked at her, she was smarter looking than myself, dress wise.

In the privacy of a closet of a public toilet, I counted my takings, and checked what stock I had left. I was amazed at the overall profit I was making at the sale of my goods, and when I thought of the way I slogged in all weathers, seven days a week delivering papers for such a paltry sum, I was determined from then on, that my father, and Karl Marx, could go to hell, for it was obvious that the world appeared to worship and respect profit makers, and I saw no reason why I should stop out in the cold. For I reasoned, that now I need only work one day a week, on a Saturday, selling firewood during the day, and domestic necessities in the evening.

I now had three bobbins of thread, four packets of pins, one packet of needles, and five pairs of laces.

Going up Percy Street, I was about to pass by the fish and chip shop, when my stomach reminded me it required attention. As I entered the shop, there was a partition on my left, and the space behind this was described as a dining room, where there were two trestle tables and forms to sit upon. The counter was so high it reminded me of a stockade, and the two ladies behind there were busy frying and had not noticed my entrance.

"Are yer there, Missis?" I called out.

One of them peered over and down on me from the high altar. "What do yer want, hinny?" she asked.

"Can I have a haddock an'chips, an plenty of batter please," said I, "To eat in th'dinin'room."

"Do yer want bread an'butter an'tea, hinny?" "I want iverythin', Missis, am clammin'," replied I. "Go an'sit down, hinny, I'll bring it in for yer." "Dining room," thought I, entering behind the partition and sitting down, "some people have fancy names for cubby holes." There was one other customer, sitting at the far table near the window; he was one of the smallest men I had ever set eyes upon, well, he was no taller than myself; and he was no dwarf either, for like myself he was equally well proportioned. Had it of been Race Week, I would have sworn he was one of the show ground midgets. "Evening," said he, the moment I showed myself, "Don't knock, just walk right in, come on, move up here beside me, and let's hear your crack." At that moment the lady brought in my supper, and I paid her, then I got cracking, but not with talk, I got on eating my fish and chips, that was the reason I had entered. I could observe, the little fellah, had just completed his own supper, and so he could very well afford to talk; he would have to wait for my contribution. Time I ate, he talked, he never ceased, he was obviously a habitual talker.

"That's right, friend, eat your grub. I can recommend the salt, and the vinegar is of vintage quality. The bread is wholesome, and the tea I've never tasted better." His small and smiling twinkling eyes were fixed firmly on me; but I did not feel he was bothering me, on the contrary, he was a pleasure to look at; I felt my gastric juices increasing abundantly merely at his presence. One thing was certain I was enjoying my fish and chips as I had never before; there was doubt in my mind that good company and good food were two of the highlights in life.

"After you have your supper, friend, come and join me in a pint of good old rare ale at the Farmers Rest," said he, continuing his one-way conversation. I took a pause in his talking as an invitation to say a few words: "I cannit gan in th'pubs, Mister, am too young," But, alas, as I talked, so did he, as though in order to convince me he had no intention of allowing me to interrupt his flow of rhetoric. "I'm not bigoted, my friend, drink or not drink, young or too old, you're welcome in my company. If you're shy or tongue-tied, don't worry in the least, I will keep the wheels of conversation going."

189

I picked up the last morsel of batter with a finger, then picked up my cup of tea, it was cold, and I silently cursed the woman who had served me; the silly bitch, pouring out one's tea before they had commenced supper, a smart housekeeper she would make.

"You've certainly enjoyed that meal, friend," remarked he, still rambling on, though it should have been obvious to him that I was taking no notice of him, for I was now too busy planning out my next port of call.

I stood up, "Av enjoyed listenin't'yer, Mister, an'I hope yer here next Saturday," thinking to myself, "because I won't be."

I left the premises, and walked down to the Kings Head.

I never set eyes upon that little man until over twenty years later, and then he didn't look a day older; but his talk was more erratic, and he had developed a pet delusion — mainly, that he was a wealthy landowner.

It was now eight twenty, and as I entered the King's Head, the mixed crowd inside were engaged in choir practice; I toted up seven songs that were being unmercilessly executed at the one time. I had no sooner commenced pushing my way through the dense packed room canvassing, when I discovered I had competition of a sort. A lady in Salvation Army uniform had entered by another door with an armful of "War Crys". She was a pretty soul, and the kind of creature one is amazed to see in such drab surroundings. It makes one think what one is prepared to do attempting to assist or smooth, another's eventual elevation to "Glory".

190

On recognising my presence, she approached me smiling, and gently patted me on the head: "Don't you think it is time you were home in bed? This is not the place for young boys." I was actually thinking myself, that it was a most unsuitable place for a refined looking young lady; but I refrained from telling her so. Had she been around during my paternal grandfather's days, and entered his pub, within seconds she would have been running out in alarm. "They al'sound well served in here, Miss, yer should sell a few papers," I remarked, intending not to discuss my activities. I have always been curious as to the various effects booze has on different individuals, ever since I was a lad. For instance in this particular pub, the men who bought something off me, rudely snubbed the Salvation lassy; who was, as I have previously mentioned, a pretty young thing, the sort of gal one could fall in love with at first sight; and the stiffs, who purchased a War Cry, waited until she was out of hearing, and advised me rudely, to piss off. However, mostly I suppose to their temporary intemperate condition, a fair number of the customers bought off one, or the other; and both of us left the pub together.

"Well, how did you get on, son?" she inquired.

I showed her my box, which by then contained only one packet of pins, and a bobbin of thread, which I had decided to keep for my mother. "Am knocking off now, Miss, av about sold out. An'I've had a gud supper of fish an'chips. If yer want t'see a midget al'dressed in green, just pop into th'fish shop up th'road."

She smiled broadly then remarked, "You're small yourself, aren't you?"

"Yes but am not goin'to stay this size al'me life, am I?" I retorted a little haughtily. At that moment she was joined by a colleague of hers who had just made his exit from another door of the pub, so I bid her goodnight, and made my way back down into Newgate Street.

As I approached the Empire music hall, I observed the kind woman wearing the remarkable hat, just coming out of the Rose and Crown with a man. They began walking down the dark alleyway alongside the Empire, so I supposed they were off to do some courting: that dead fox round her neck, would feel at home down there.

Suddenly my attention was drawn to the sound of a commotion from the other side of the road, the bar door had been slammed open and two men sprawled out and began setting about each other with their fists. Close on their heels, came out about a dozen other men, not to separate the combatants it appeared, but to encourage them on. Each one of them calling out advice to their particular favourite: "Sock him, Sid, with yer fist, yer idiot." "Go on poke him in th'eye, Sid." "Use yer head, Bob, it's hard enough."

A group of women passing by stopped in their tracks and began screaming their heads off, instead of moving on. Within a few minutes another four men joined in, kicking, and punching, and soon the whole crowd were on the tramlines ignoring an approaching tram clanging the warning bell. Then the sound of another bell came from the direction of nearby Grainger Street, and a

Black Maria, veered round the corner. It screeched to a halt, the back doors of the large van flew open, and a number of Bobbies jumped out and joined in the conflict. To me it appeared, those individuals who were receiving the heaviest pounding from the law, fought all the more furiously, as though encouraged by rough usage. Finally, those who regained their senses quick enough, broke loose from the melee, and ran like hell up Newgate Street and out of sight. But five slow witted one's were thrown bodily into the Police van, as though they were redundant tailors dummies. And once more peace returned to Newgate Street.

Now that the entertainment was over, I went round the corner and caught a tram to Benwell. Once again, the conductor insisted that I remain downstairs, which was full of pub crawlers, making a nuisance to passengers who were either too young to drink, or too hard-up to afford it.

Some of them were attempting to sing, or doing their utmost to encourage others to try; while others were creating an unpleasant smell with their eating of cowheels, tripe, and fish and chips.

I jumped off at my stop, grateful to escape from the noise and the offensive smell.

My mother was sitting by the fire; no signs of my father, so I placed all of my profits on to the table, and told my mother how I had come by the money. I placed the packet of pins and the bobbin of thread in her lap, and apparently she was in the act of warning me with her eyes, when my father came out of the bedroom. I received a sharp clip over the ear, and a warning of what I would get if I done the like again.

So much for my attempt to embark on a future of private enterprise!

CHAPTER
THIRTEEN

I Leave School

When my twelfth birthday had arrived I had thought my previous life to have been a very long one; but when one arrives at a certain age, I think time appears to pass by at an accelerated speed; thus to me, the next two years went by on wings. When the school broke up for the summer holidays in 1938, the day I thought I had been yearning for arrived. I was fourteen years old and now I was free at last from the tyranny of the wasteful elementary education machine.

Of course, had I been aware as to what my future hardships, and prospects were to be, I would have begged of my father, and of my headmaster, to allow me to remain at school, secure in that haven of make-believe.

Now in place of summer weeks of freedom to play at cowboys, on Geordie Goddards field, or on the quarry behind the Grand cinema, I had in the face of stiff competition, to seek full-time work!

To my often previous requests that I be given the opportunity of wearing long trousers, the reply from my father, who had to take into consideration the cost of procuring them, had always been: "When you leave

195

school son." Well, I had left school, and I was excited with the thrill of learning that I would have a pair of long trousers in time to seek work on the Monday. On the Saturday evening I witnessed, to my horror, my mother cutting down and altering, a pair of my father's work-day trousers; he having gained another pair for himself on his tatting round. Growing up or not, I went to bed weeping.

On the Monday, dressed in my father's rejected trousers, I left the house to begin my quest for work. I almost slinked down that street, for I am sure there couldn't have been a more self-conscious creature on earth that morning. I was aware of the many amusing glances being cast on me from the neighbours standing in the street, but it was left to the kids who were gathered there, as though expecting to witness some ridiculous spectacle, to loudly proclaim how I looked, and indeed how I felt: "Hey, Tommy — you've got yer father's troosers on, what a bloody mess yer look." For the first time since I could remember, I galloped down the street and I was not pretending to be one of my favourite western heroes on his horse, I was simply running away out of sight.

After a thorough search I eventually observed in a grocer's shop window a card advertising for a "Smart Strong Errand-Boy". Without a moment's hesitation I entered the shop and applied for the job. I informed the manager, that I was one of the strongest and fastest kids in the neighbourhood. With unemployment being so high, I was obviously determined to impress the manager; and I succeeded for he offered me the job.

The very next morning in the shop the manager convinced me that he had believed me quite sincerely the day before, when I had boasted about my strength. He ordered me to go out into the backyard and take out the carrier cycle into the lane where it could be loaded up with grocery orders. Whoever invented the commercial carrier cycle, may have been a clever sort of man; though to be honest, when I set eyes upon the machine that I was expected to use, I was of the immediate opinion, that whoever had built this ugly huge machine, ought to have kept it for his own use, or presented it to some industrial museum. Although it was a machine of uncertain age, and mainly kept together by numerous bindings of old wire, nevertheless, I was convinced it would have even been a cycle difficult to manoeuvre from the day it had been manufactured.

The manager and his assistant came out into the lane as I was placing the bike up on its stand. "Get up on to the bike," said the manager, "And we'll load up the carrier for you." So I climbed up on to the seat; and I mean climb; when I was sitting on it, my toes just about reached the pedals. Both of them began packing parcels into the large carrier basket; the assistant manager, a young, good-looking chap, and undoubtedly possessing more foresight, and consideration, than his senior colleague, suggested to him, not to fill the basket too much, but in vain. So I mildly remarked, that I would have to be able to see where I was going, which would be difficult if they piled up the packages any higher.

197

"Well, Tich," said the dry looking unhumorous manager, after placing the last order on top, "They're all for Pendower estate." And with his foot, he kicked up the cycle stand into the clips that secured it. Instantly, the back wheel lifted up, in the fashion one could say, of a playful filly who was objecting to the weight of its rider. The packages flew in all directions; fortunately for me, I went only in one direction and in one piece, and escaped with nothing but a bruised knee. I was thankful to survive this unprovoked assassination attempt of this grocer-manager, but I decided he was one whom I would have to watch carefully in the future. Time he concerned himself mainly with the parcels of groceries on the roadway, the assistant, had ran back into the shop and returned with the first aid box, and attended to my knee.

I suggested to the manager, that he allow me to decide what weight I could handle with safety; for as I pointed out, being a quick walker, and a fast runner, it should be obvious I would be a swift cyclist; he reluctantly agreed to my proposal.

However, I must state, this was the first time on any cycle in my life; and I wish to take this opportunity to warn any prospective errand-boy, not to attempt to learn the skill of cycling on a carrier-bike, especially so when it's loaded with merchandise; and the machine perhaps being held together by means of wire salvaged from Danish egg boxes, or any other box for that matter.

"Keep looking straight ahead son, and keep your eyes off the front wheel," were the parting words of the assistant manager. I learned later that it was sound advice; but at that particular time, his counsel had me concerned no-end, for any minute on my travels I was expecting the front wheel to drop off; but as I was cycling up Pendower Way, it was the chain that fell off, in two pieces. In twenty minutes, I proved to myself that I probably possessed some mechanical skill by fixing it.

At my first call, I was met on the doorway with an angry looking woman, holding a bulging eyed Pekinese in her arms, and she gave me a dressing down for being late, and for having dirty hands. I attempted to explain about the cycle chain, which had resulted in both delay and with staining my hands. But this only incensed her. I came to the conclusion after many such experiences, that many adults did not wish to listen to explanations from a young person, whom they were in the midst of chastising, rightly or wrongly; indeed I often found myself being accused of rudeness in answering back.

When I arrived back at the shop, I discovered she had been on the phone complaining to the manager about my being late, and with having dirty hands. He did not wish to listen to explanations. In my opinion, the cycle was falling apart, nevertheless, I had to be the scapegoat in order to conceal the fact. I remarked to the assistant, "That a whole day at the poss-tub, would do her the world of good, in place of nursing her little squeaky fat Pekinese," and he agreed with my sentiments.

There was a young girl who served in the shop, a year older than myself, pretty too. She was forever smiling and winking at me whenever I happened to be around, and at first I ignored her advances, thinking she would do likewise as a result, but I was proved wrong. Now it was my task to weigh, and bag the flour and sugar which always arrived in bulk; and she began practising the enticing habit of coming into the back shop whilst I was attending to those jobs, and pretend to be reaching for some commodity on the shelves above my head, and of course pressed herself real close to me; then perhaps attend to her garters. I think I was a little alarmed at her coquetry, and puzzled as to what sort of response was expected of me. I had always played at cowboys, with the lads in my spare time; I think I was cowboy mad; and girls for some reason never played cowboys, least not where I lived, so therefore I had no previous experience whatsoever of flirtation. Though mind you, I have already admitted to having a real crush on a girl named Anne, who lived on the terrace. I looked upon her as my ideal dream girl, but there was no flirtation unfortunately. I think she was aware of my feelings towards her, but no doubt she was equally aware how shy and tongue-tied I was in her presence, so nothing came of it.

This girl working with me in the grocer's shop, also realised I was terribly shy, but she appeared determined to do something about it. Soon she had me kissing and hugging her close, yet still I resisted. Why on earth she wasted her talent and charms on such a dreamer as myself, I never could tell, but she kept trying, much to my secret delight.

On Tyneside, in winter, one can always rely on experiencing a fair amount of Eskimo scenery, and so when the snow lay too deep for cycling then I had to load up the large clumsy delivery barrow, which ran on heavy wheels encircled with a metal rim, and haul it along the terrace and up steep hills, real heavy work. Even the many cart horses that passed me on my travels usually jerked their heads around to stare at me in surprise; even though they themselves were working every bit as hard as myself.

Monday was the day when fresh stock of provisions arrived. The small items such as tins of biscuits, and packages containing condiments, were no problem at all; but I think my future chest and shoulder muscle developments, and most probably irreparable spinal disabilities, could be attributed to the humping of hundredweight sacks of sugar and flour, from the van parked in the back lane, through the backyard and up the steps into the back shop; no light task for a fourteen year old boy. If custom was not too brisk at such times, then usually the assistant manager would help me, time the manager stood by checking the goods in; but often as not, I unloaded the van on my own.

As regarding the Shop Hours Act for Young Persons, my governor appeared to be apathetic towards it; not only was I sometimes kept after my hours in the evening if things were busy, but he robbed me of a number of my half day holidays, yet never once did he add another penny to my weekly wage of seven and sixpence. I often debated with myself what reason there was for working so hard, and so long hours, when in actual fact neither my parents or myself were financially better off than we had been when I was delivering newspapers and selling firewood? However, be as it may, I was reminded that full-time employment, if one could obtain it, was the expected norm of anyone on leaving school.

One particular Wednesday, when I ought to have finished work at one o'clock, I was still at it pulling the barrow through the snow until nearly four in the afternoon. When I arrived home, my father decided he would act as my unofficial shop steward.

The next morning he called into the shop and gave the manager a right dressing down, and to my surprise, the assistant manager took sides with my father.

As a result of this incident, I was transferred to another branch further along the terrace towards the direction of the city. Apart from missing the hugging and kissing of sweet Jennie, it soon became obvious to me, within hours of joining this other branch, that the manager of it must have been advised to work me a penneth. The delivery barrow that was loaded up for me to haul through the snow was even larger and heavier than the former, and he appeared to overload it deliberately. I was amazed at his pettiness considering it was my nature to go out of my way to please, whoever was employing me at any particular time, no matter how difficult the work.

Within two weeks I decided there was no alternative but to hand in my notice. When I received my insurance card on leaving, I concealed it in one of my shoes, and refrained from mentioning to my parents that I had packed my job in, for life was hard enough without running the risk of creating a domestic riot; I would have to chance to luck in finding another job and a wage for the following week.

Once more on a Monday morning I left the house at my usual time with my bait, and my insurance card concealed down one of my stockings.

On Sunday, I had discovered a couple of building sites on Geordie Goddard's field at the end of Elm Street, near Jennings the bakery. Practically all the local allotments on the field had now unfortunately been taken over by the builders, which brought to an end the pleasure, and the means of growing desperately needed vegetables by many a local unemployed man.

Needless to say from my point of view, and from many others in the district, the houses being built on the sites of the former allotments were nothing to do with much required slum clearance, for they were all to be private houses for sale.

By nine o'clock, I had found work on one of the two sites, as a can-boy. The day went quietly enough: but I somehow sensed it was a day of weighing-up; and I was the one being weighed-up, by all the comics, and smart alicks on the job. But I was confident enough; one does not commence delivering and selling newspapers, firewood, and hawk small domestic items around city pubs, without becoming acquainted with all types of leg-pullers, and eccentrics. So on the very next day, when these notorious characters got cracking, I had their number all right, but I was sufficiently wise enough to act a little simple, for I had learned the hard way that most of these adult leg-pullers, do not take too kindly to nippers who appear to be too smart.

About nine o'clock, a particular joiner ordered me to go over to the stores cabin and search around for the left-handed hammer, and vaguely described it. Now at this stage in my life, I had just ceased reading comics, and had begun interesting myself in books, and that very morning I had placed a book in my coat pocket to read during my lunch hour. The storeman, as was expected of him, kept a straight face when I declared to him what I had come for. "I'm going round the site, nipper, to check on what stock I have out, so have a careful look around for it." And off he went, no doubt to report to the joiner who had sent me. No sooner had he gone, than out came my book, and I sat down to read for a while. After what I considered to be a reasonable absence I returned to the joiner who was working among a number of other men and sadly informed him that the left-handed hammer was nowhere to be found, and I pretended to look very surprised when everyone within hearing began laughing their heads off. In the afternoon one of the bricklayers sent me off to search around the site, for the "Long Stand". Once out of sight of him, I entered one of the completed houses where no one was present at that moment, and enjoyed the "long-sit-down", much more comfortable than a "long-stand" in a dirty cold cabin.

On the Friday I received my eight shillings wages, an increase of sixpence from my previous job, and not as much gut-straining into the bargain. On the Saturday morning, after tea break, the joiner who had set the ball rolling, by sending me off to search for the left-handed hammer, took off his cap and told me to accompany him round the site: "Cum on, lads, remember the can-lad." and he set the collection off by placing a threepenny piece into his cap for me; only a minority of the men offered some excuse for not contributing; but I respected their excuse for they had kids of their own to think about. Of course this pleasant ritual came as a complete surprise to me; when the collection had been toted-up, I found I was six and ninepence better off. "Thanks very much, mister," said I gratefully to the joiner. "Ah that's nowt tich, hinny, it's a pleasure," replied he.

Even my father treated me with reverence that particular weekend; I was now a fully fledged working man.

One morning after having been around the site and collected the men's money for their cigarettes, a shifty looking bricklayer came up to me and handed me a slip of paper which had five or six numbers wrote upon it. "Here, Tich," said he abruptly, "Buy al'the fags at the Co-op and hand this number in, and bring back the check to me."

"Bloody cheek," thought I, for he was one of the few who seldom gave me any can-money, yet I always done more errands for him than any other man on the job, furthermore, he was single, and in a better fix than the married men; no wonder he was looked upon as a near relation to Ebenezer Scrooge.

A week later, a certain labourer requested me also to purchase the fags at the co-op, on his own number.

"Am sorry, Bob," replied I, "I wish yer had of spoken a week ago, Scrooge, the bricky, makes me get th'fags at the co-op on his number."

"Never mind tich, hinny, it's not your fault," said he.

On my way to the co-op, I debated the issue with myself. "Now the labourer was a married man with four children, yet he still gave me can-money on a Saturday morning." So I got the fags on his number.

Back on the job I gave the check to Bob. "Here, Bob, I got your number; to hell with crafty Frank, I'll poison his tea if I git any nonsense oot of him."

"If the queer fellow gives you any trouble tich, tell me, I'll land him one," replied Bob.

Not another penny can-money did I ever get from poor frustrated Frank. I am sure, if I had been a little older he would have challenged me to a scrap; and I suppose I would have accepted. From that day onwards, he rewarded me with nothing but surly looks, and every time he passed by me, he would distinctly mutter, "You little renegade, toe-rag, you've had it from me, boy."

On this building site I was learning something fresh every day, mostly on the oddities of human nature. For instance, until a certain incident one day, I never knew such a character as a bait snatcher existed; I had always thought previously that only mice and rats pinched grub.

One particular day at noon, when the whistle blew, and the men streamed into the cabin for their can of tea, one of the men discovered that his bait had vanished; no doubt he must have had something extra special for lunch, for I suppose the thief must have done a little exploring around, according to the comments from a number of the men. It was a difficult problem to find out whoever may be responsible, for on most building sites, the men will collect their can of tea from a central point, then go off to their favourite spot to have their lunch.

Even massings of tea and sugar vanished at times. So the bait cabin was kept locked, and the pilfering ceased. I suppose whoever had been helping themselves, had then to learn to spend more on grub, and less on bass.

One Saturday morning, an over-dressed woman, wearing rings on practically every finger of both hands, came up to me and inquired for the whereabouts of a particular chap. I told her I would go off and search for him; now he was a character who seldom appeared to have either bait, or Woodbines. I discovered him stuffing firewood into his haversack, and informed him that I thought his wife was looking for him. He peered at me suspiciously, probably wondering, whether one of the leg-pullers, had put me up to it. But his reluctance to believe me changed instantly, and his face turned a crimson colour, not only through embarrassment I suppose, but through temper, when he observed the over-dressed woman, who had followed me, approaching him. He began walking down the road away from her, intending that she should follow, thus not having his affairs discussed in my hearing. But apparently she was in no mood for considering his feelings, and in a clear audible tone, began reading him, her version of the "riot act", warning him in no

207

uncertain high-handed manner. Desperately he handed her some money, hoping to quieten her; she accepted it, and gave him more advice, before walking away. Another workman who was witnessing the scene, mischievously called out, "Cum an'have a look lads, the money lender is after shifty Sam." A smile broke out over the hard face of the money-lender as she went down the road, but there was no sign of humour on the face of the debtor, who scowled at his tormentor, and made off to conceal his discomfort.

A month later, the job came to an end, only the painters remained, and as they had an apprentice to attend to their wants, I got the push, along with the majority of the workmen, on the Friday evening.

I was not destined to be idle long. On the following Monday, leaving home at the usual time, I met my friend the joiner walking along Gill Street. "Hellow, Tich, going to look for werk, son? Cum with me, I might git yer a start." Not far from our last job was another site, and so we headed for it. By the time the eight o'clock whistle blew, both of us were on the pay-sheet. After building up my fire, I collected up all the men's cans, and decided to clean them with sand, for some of them resembled miniature unscoured sewage pans. Came the morning tea break, I handed each man his sparkling clean can full of hot tea. To my amazement, one of the plasterers, a small fat man, came charging back to me, cursing out loud. "Yer silly little waster — it tuk me months to git me can seasoned as it was; ah cannit taste th'tea noo."

From that moment the poor little fat man took a terrible dislike to me. He would not even ask me to go a message for him, such was his aversion towards me, since I had cleaned his tea-can. One morning as I was passing through one of the houses under construction, and where he was busy plastering the walls, he turned towards me and said. "You little varlet, I have never had a gud night's sleep since yer came on to the job."

I was at a loss as to what he expected me to do about it, so I went on my way collecting the men's cans.

As I presumed beforehand, the usual leg-pullers were on the job; and within hours of having started on the site, they were competing with one another in order to get a kick out of wasting my time by sending me off to search for some ridiculous non-existent item, such as the "long-stand, wire netting oilcan, a cap full of nail holes, cans of colourless paint, left handed hammer"; the list was endless.

When I was not making tea, or running errands I went out of my way to make myself useful, having at the back of my mind that I could perhaps learn some form of construction skill that would ensure me regular employment; though little did I know then of the building trade set-up, of the permanent insecurity, where a man could be given one hour's notice and sent packing, without any kind of redress. But another reason for seeking out jobs to do, was that I was completely unacquainted with idleness. I took a hand at painting, nailed laths on the partition walls for the plasterers, mixed compo for the bricklayers, and dug ditches for the plumbers.

The son of my employer, was a really nice chap, open and honest, and I got on very well with him. But with his old man, well I always ensured that I was extra busy, or out of sight when he was around. He was one of the most embittered and sarcastic employers I have ever come across. A number of times I witnessed him arrive on the site a little the worse for drink, and then all the men were on their toes.

On reflection, I am of the opinion, that he was one of those unfortunate individuals who ought to have never been introduced to alcohol, for he was extremely moody without it, but once he was on it, it appeared to depress him to a very low degree. How I come to this conclusion is, a few years later, I met him a number of times drinking in a particular public house, and I always got on talking to him; without of course letting on that I once worked for him, and I always discovered that as the night progressed, and as his alcohol intake increased, he became sullen, then so depressed, that anyone of understanding could only feel sorry for him. His condition must have been pathological, for there was no other explanation for his behaviour. He lived in a nice house; the building trade was picking-up, and his son, was attending to all the administration and supervising of the work that was necessary.

March came along, and although the snow was still around, a number of the houses near completion required clearing of rubble, and cleaning out, so none of us were in danger of being made idle. Nevertheless, I was being cautious, and for three nights running I had been out selling "Evening Chronicle Special" on the

Munich crisis, so I felt confident that if I were to be laid off through bad weather, I would be able to continue earning a wage by clearing snow from the pathways of the nearby private houses, and with selling "Specials" in the evening.

One thing was certain, I had now to look upon myself as a regular wage-earner, and the family budget was now dependant on my income however small it was, and I was confident it would take more than the elements to hold me back from raising a few bob.

One Friday afternoon a lorry load of cement arrived on the site. Although it was no concern of mine, I joined in and assisted in unloading it. After the task was complete, I sat down where I was for a rest; of course I ought to have concealed myself. The next thing I was aware of, was the boss tapping me on the head with a pencil: "Think I pay you just to make a few cans of tea, then sit on your backside the rest of the day?" he growled. I attempted to explain that I had been helping to unload cement not over five minutes earlier. "Don't argue with me, you little bugger — you're fired."

So that was that, who was I to deny him his democratic rights?

I learned later that his son, who had been absent at the time I was sacked, had argued like hell with his father for stooping to such an act. Good for him, for I am always grateful for any consideration directed towards justice.

The following week I became a butcher's errand boy. No time wasted with me when it came to wage earning and helping to make ends meet.

Within two hours of being shown the know-how, I was making sausages like an expert; whether they were fit for human consumption is another matter! My new employer was a one-man firm, and he informed me at the beginning, he had to be able to rely on his errand boy being swift, and quick-witted. Well, I was of the opinion that no errand boy was swifter than myself, and he soon taught me what being quick-witted meant, by his terms. From the worn-out fridge, he brought out two large enamel dishes of seedy looking meat scraps, and a small dish of sausage skins, which were green in colour instead of being white. Handing me an empty lemonade bottle and threepence, he directed me to go to the chemist along the road and purchase threepenneth of "Doctor". On the way, I had it in the back of my mind, that the boss was perhaps no different from the leg-pullers on the building sites, and was deliberately sending me on a fool's errand; if so, I was not complaining, it was his pay-time that was being wasted not mine: sufficient to say, I was dubious. But at the chemist's the assistant took my bottle, went behind the prescription partition, and soon returned with my bottle two thirds full of a colourless liquid resembling water. On my return to the shop, the boss poured a small amount of this liquid over the sausage skins; in about five minutes those skins were bleached white. One dish of the meat scraps were put through the mincer, then he sprinkled a fair amount of the "Doctor" over it, and to my amazement, the meat took on a natural healthy colour and it smelt fresh too. Following his instructions I took over the operation,

212

added the other usual ingredients, being a little heavy-handed on the seasoning, mixed it up into a dough, and then through the sausage machine it went. That liquid was not called "Doctor" for nothing; it certainly gave the Harley Street treatment to the sausage meat. But young as I was then, I would not have fed a stray cat on the finished product.

Next, my boss instructed me on how to make potted meat. In the back shop there was an old boiler, similar to the type found in many of the backyards of the district, which were used by the tenants to do their washing in. I cut up the scraps of meat from the second container, poured some "Doctor" over it, and tipped the lot into the boiler.

It is surprising what cooking will conceal to some degree. Within two hours of boiling, the boss declared that the meat was cooked. I scooped this mess out and filled up a number of small enamel dishes. After cooling I placed them all in the fridge, such as it was.

The next morning, these dishes of meat were placed in the window, with a card displaying in large bold letters "Freshly Made Potted Meat".

If anyone reading this assumes that the meat treatment I have described above was solely the speciality of this one-man firm, let me state that, a few months later, I was employed as an errand-boy at a branch of one of the largest chain-butchers in the country, and the same unappetising methods were practised there also. One must remember, in many of the shops in those days, refrigeration was often in a backward state; nevertheless despite this drawback which prevented some foods from being kept wholesome over the weekend, nothing whatsoever was wasted in the butchering trade; and Monday morning was the obvious day for any weekend waste to be processed.

Apart from the humanitarian feelings that individuals like Shelley and Shaw had towards the animal Kingdom, I for one could appreciate their conversion to vegetarianism!

When I was introduced to the butcher's carrier-bike, I was instantly reminded of the bone-shaker belonging to my first employer, and I could only assume that no new carrier-cycles had been manufactured for the past two or three decades. From the day I commenced work there, until the day I left, I was kept busy repairing punctures, patching up the tyres, fixing the brakes, and securing the seat and mudguards with lengths of twine and wire.

I gathered early on, that my boss was just about scraping through financially on a week-to-week basis.

To his credit, he never kept me over my hours, nor did he ever rob me of a half day holiday.

Within a few weeks of Britain declaring war, about two thirds of my employer's customers departed into the countryside in order to escape from the possible risk of air raids. The result of this sudden exodus decided him that he had no alternative but to close-up shop.

My mother, brothers, and two younger sisters, were also evacuated; leaving behind my father, my elder sister, and myself. It was then, when there were only three of us left at home, that the housing department presented us with a six room council house in the suburbs; with a back garden almost large enough for to land a Spitfire on.

For the first time in my life, I had a room to myself as well as a whole double bed, in which I could toss and turn whenever I felt like it and not to be told to lie still, and no feet in my face. For weeks afterwards, my father had to come into my bedroom and literally haul me out of bed in the mornings in order to get me to work on time, such was the way in which sudden dreamland luxury affected me.

Searching for and commencing new jobs was becoming one of my regular occupations. On the following Monday, I began work in a branch shop of a firm of chain-butchers. It was my fifth job in eighteen months, since leaving school, though the job-drifting was through no fault of my own; not one piece of advice nor any guidance did I receive from any quarter as to whether I ought to serve my time in some trade, and thus escape from becoming a confirmed drifter, compelled to seek and accept any dead-end and unrenumerative occupation.

There is nothing like being reared in the abyss, to condition one to accept their lot; which is usually in the form of restricted living space; a deficient diet; and an inferior type of education.

Of course being imaginative like most young boys, and furthermore being a willing worker, I wasted no time bemoaning my luck; I possessed a fine singing voice, and so I was forever consoling myself, that when I grew up, I would seek an audition, become a celebrated singer, and thus be in a position to eat my fill; purchase clothes other than from the second-hand shops; and who knows get myself a belated education.

But alas, the hopeful day-dreams of the young very seldom materialise. I did not land upon the stage as a singer, but during my continuation of drifting from job to job, I did land upon the road as a hobo.

I had learned one time at school that the reason for much unemployment, and resulting lack of prosperity, was due to the country's National Debt. My father, apparently, had no respect for that line of reasoning. When in April 1939, he was found work in Vickers Armstrongs on Scotswood Road, with the assurance of all the overtime he could wish for, his first job for ten years, he knew that employment had only been found for him and others in a similar plight, after having been left idle on the dole for years, solely on account that the "war drums" were beginning to be tuned up. "You mark my words, son," said he, on obtaining the job, "Before long the Government will print all the money they require, and won't care two-bob for their so-called National Debt."

So ends the story of my childhood, the writing of which I have intended doing since I was a young man. It is the story I have written in my mind countless times, reminiscing over each little detail. Odd as it may seem to some, even the memories of one's childhood hardships are worth holding on to, for such experiences have assisted in moulding one's character, whether for good, or ill.

ISIS publish a wide range of books in large print, from fiction to biography. Any suggestions for books you would like to see in large print or audio are always welcome. Please send to the Editorial department at:

ISIS Publishing Ltd.
7 Centremead
Osney Mead
Oxford OX2 0ES
(01865) 250 333

A full list of titles is available free of charge from:
Ulverscroft large print books

(UK)
The Green
Bradgate Road, Anstey
Leicester LE7 7FU
Tel: (0116) 236 4325

(Australia)
P.O Box 953
Crows Nest
NSW 1585
Tel: (02) 9436 2622

(USA)
1881 Ridge Road
P.O Box 1230, West Seneca,
N.Y. 14224-1230
Tel: (716) 674 4270

(Canada)
P.O Box 80038
Burlington
Ontario L7L 6B1
Tel: (905) 637 8734

(New Zealand)
P.O Box 456
Feilding
Tel: (06) 323 6828

Details of **ISIS** complete and unabridged audio books are also available from these offices. Alternatively, contact your local library for details of their collection of **ISIS** large print and unabridged audio books.